Life's Answer

Creating Your World
Through Positive Thought

Also available by Beth and Lee McCain

BOOKS BY BETH AND LEE McCAIN
A Grateful Life: Living the Law of Attraction
Transcripts from the Core Being
The Universal Law of Attraction Resource Book
The Law of Attraction Guided Journal
Unlimited Thoughts
Law of Attraction Courses for Your Success
Violet's Wish

FEATURE FILM ON DVD
Beyond the Law of Attraction

CD AND mp3 AUDIO DOWNLOADS
THE KEY SERIES:
Unlocking the Secret to The Secret
Career
Relationships
Financial Abundance
Confidence
Weight Loss
Connect with the Universe
LOA for Guys Only
LOA for Kids
Stop the Struggle
Beth and Lee on the Road (Live appearances)

A GRATEFUL LIFE BOOK

Published by the Grateful Life Company
An imprint of The BLM Creative Work Shoppe
1056 Green Acres Road, No. 102-237
Eugene, Oregon 97408 USA

First edition: June 2009

Library of Congress Cataloging-in-Publication Data

McCain, Beth 1962—
McCain, Lee 1961—

Life's Answer / Beth & Lee McCain.— 1st ed.

p.   cm.

ISBN 1-442-17290-8   EAN-13 9-781442-172906

1. Self improvement.   2. Positive Thought.

3. Metaphysical studies and practices.

I.   Title

Printed in the United States of America

Published simultaneously in Canada, the United Kingdom, and Australia

10 9 8 7 6 5 4 3 2 1

Life's Answer

Creating Your World
Through Positive Thought

Beth and Lee McCain

Grateful Life Press

www.bethandleemccain.com

For the positive thinker
who resides in each one of us.

Table of Contents

CHAPTER ONE

Positive Thought Will Change your Life

How Positive Thought Works

Our whole lives revolve around thought; everything that we do and everything that we are is comprised of thoughts and feelings. Each day thousands of thoughts run through our heads and we think nothing of it and when life goes awry we blame it on luck or on the powers from above. Life seems unfair and we quickly exhibit the mentality of *Why does everyone but me get what they want?*

Changing your way of thinking will change your life. Are you wondering how just changing your way of thought can direct your whole life to having everything that you have always wanted? It will definitely take some determination on your part but you can have the life you want and all the things that go with it. All it takes is a positive attitude and positive thoughts to enable it all to come true for you.

Everything you can see, feel, taste, hear, or touch on this earth is made from the same substance. Some are solid and fixed and some are in a state of constant change but each substance is made of one thing — energy. As we think about each of the above, we can see that they cross from the visible to the invisible but all are still created from the same substance.

When we reach the invisible we find the substance of All in the purest state. Everything is made of energy. Each thought, each force of Nature, even the chair you sit on is made of energy; the same energy, it just vibrates at a different rate.

When you think, you are sending out vibrations that are real. These vibrations manifest as heat, electricity, light, and magnetism. Just because you can't see or taste them does not mean that they are any less real. A magnet can send out vibrations and create such a force that it can attract a piece of steel weighing a much larger ratio compared to its own weight. You cannot see the magnet actually drawing the steel to it, but it happens nevertheless even if you don't see it with the naked eye.

This is how what we think and feel affects everyday life. We emit vibrations that return to us through the Universe in some kind of form. The most powerful energy can come from nature, and this energy is usually manifested as an invisible force. We, as humans, are also a powerful source of energy and, again, our energy appears for the most part in an invisible form.

Human thought is the power of the Universe working through man. Thought is energy and energy is what makes up everything. And while everything is made of the same energy, everything vibrates at a different speed. Thoughts can create negative circumstances just as easily as positive ones, and when we consciously or unconsciously visualize any kind of lack, we grow these circumstances.

When you toss a stone into a still lake you can clearly see the ripples that are emitted. Imagine the rock as a thought; that thought produces ripples that spread out producing even more ripples.

Our thoughts extend as if in an ocean of thoughts within our world, moving in different directions reproduced by the intensity and repetition of focus that you put into them. Someone who has a strong thought and feeling surrounded by confidence and joy won't be affected by the strong thoughts and feelings of failure or doubt.

Conversely, someone who is having negative thoughts will not be affected by positive thought. If the person focusing on negative thoughts changes them to the positive they will then become affected by positive thoughts which will continue to reproduce bringing more of the same.

As we go about life we also tend to attract to us others of the same intense thoughts we tend to repeat in our own daily lives. Someone who thinks success will begin to draw in the minds of others who are thinking likewise and they will help one another. This usually happens unconsciously. Through auto-pilot thinking we sometimes don't realize that each person in our life is a reflection of our own thoughts. Therefore, if the mind is constantly thinking of failure it will draw to it like minded people who also embrace failure.

When you are thinking positive thoughts you are sending out vibrations that will affect not only you, but others as well. The more you emit these vibrations the more of the same will come your way. It is inevitable.

Not only does each thought of significance bring others to you but the thought has a drawing power that attracts to us not only thoughts but circumstances, people, and things. For instance, thoughts of joy and love bring you like circumstances as well as people and things to love.

Thoughts of hate only attract more to hate. This is why it is so important to change your way of thinking in life and this is what will change everything about your life. Man is the only creature on earth that makes his own negative surroundings and then will blame others for it, when in actuality he has just attracted it to himself.

Gratitude is one of the primary movers in changing your life through positive thought. First, believe in one All — one intelligent substance, God, however you define it; something that all things proceed through. Then you will see that this substance can bring you everything you desire and actually gave you the ability to make it happen. When acknowledging this, relate yourself to your ability and the energy that runs through you and everything on this planet; be grateful for everything that is around you.

Be grateful that you have this ability instead of cursing it or not knowing about it.

The more you fix your mind on the good things that come to you, the more good will actually come. Exhibit mental gratitude for life. This puts your mind in closer connection with the source of the energy and blessings. A grateful mind continually expects good things and through that expectation more good things come. Every wave of gratefulness helps increase your personal belief that life is going just as you have envisioned. And even if it doesn't go exactly as you thought, being grateful and expecting more good causes it all to arrive via the Universe eventually.

Another method of demonstrating your gratefulness is to give others more of value than what you perceive that you will ever receive from them. If you are paying a bill take the extra step and talk to the employee taking your money. Don't be resentful and imagine how you wish you didn't have to pay the bill; rather, pay it forward through your positive actions.

Give the clerk a smile.

Cut her a break if she is in a bad mood.

Once you begin the auto-process of kindness by giving more, you will soon see the benefits that you will reap. You will find that by focusing on the positive, even in a Force-10 storm of negativity, you will have lesser negatives in your life to be concerned about. Every experience that you have is just as valuable as the next one whether it may seem negative or positive. You can always learn from the experience. All experiences contain wisdom but there is no reason to repeat over and over again the experiences that may have been negative.

As you repeatedly mull over a negative experience remember that you are focusing and thinking about the past, and this will attract back to you with the very thoughts and energy that you are emitting. The experience may not arrive exactly as before but it will create the same feelings and thoughts surrounding the previous experience. Just see what you have learned, if anything, and then move on to bigger and better things.

Sometimes people elect to shut their eyes to the past negatives or the future but believe in them just the same. Know that ignoring these feelings and thoughts will not make them go away. But contemplating on any particular experience and then moving on from it will keep that experience from coming back to you. And if you dread your future, it will as quickly materialize into the kind of future you are focusing on. Half the battle is recognizing your train of thought and then changing it to the positive.

Begin to recognize the buildup that culminates in a bad day and then ask yourself what triggers bad days. Such days are usually borne of frustration, lack of appreciation, feeling forced to do what you don't want to do, others around you feeling bad, disappointment, an unexpected change of plans, collective weather, neighbors, or piles of bills just to name a few. Sound familiar?

Recognize when the build is rising within you and defuse it. When you recognize such feelings when they are small, they will be easier to defuse. But if you wait too long, you will end up creating that hard day that you have been so trying to avoid. And again, if your day just feels like one of those days, ride it with ease and know that the next day will be better.

We will sometimes enjoy an excellent day and then forget to be grateful for it. You will want to be grateful on these excellent days as well as the harder days because both will attract more to be grateful for. Recognize whenever you have an exceptional day and thank the Universe repeatedly for the wonderful day that you have just created.

As far as we are concerned, your perception is a key component when applying the Law of Attraction. We have been taught to believe exactly what we see or what we 'think' we see. It's important to begin to realize that just because you see something it doesn't always mean that that is exactly how it is.

Here's an example: Everyday you see the same gentleman on your way to work and he is always at the bus stop. He carries a cheap little umbrella that has a broken spoke and he wears the same hat time and time again. Your perception of this gentleman may be that you think he must be financially poor because he rides the bus, wears the same hat daily, and carries a broken umbrella. This is your perception.

But you really have no idea who this man is, and you think you see he doesn't have much. Think about this for a moment. You have just made a judgment through your own perception and have made the assumption that he has no money. Each morning you feel sorry for the little man with his broken umbrella and one day you decide to buy him a new umbrella.

You leave a little earlier and head to the bus stop. There he is, all by himself, with his broken umbrella. You introduce yourself telling him that you see him every morning and thought he could use a newer umbrella. He smiles very kindly and refuses your gift. He explains that his wife had given him that umbrella, had recently passed on, and that he used to ride the bus with her each morning simply because they enjoyed taking the ride together.

So it was now clear that each morning he was riding the bus with his broken umbrella to enjoy the memories of his wife. He said he missed her so much and this daily constitutional eased his pain. You learn later that he parks his car — a Jaguar XJS — every morning by the bus stop and rides for a few hours, then climbs back in his car and drives to his Park Avenue home. Do you see what your perception/assumption did? It was dead wrong. Never take anything at face value.

Unless you have walked in someone else's shoes, you have no idea what they have been through. *This also goes for the Universe.*

Just because something appears to be one way, doesn't mean it is. There are many ways of every possibility throughout the Universe and there is constant invisible energy working for you within the Universe. When you feel like there is no movement in your life whether it is attracting more money, a relationship, or better health, remember that it is only the outer appearance that you are seeing through the guise of your normal perception.

Nothing ever sits still. Even if you can't see it with your eyes, there is constant movement. If you do your part by thinking and feeling each of your purposes and your desires, the Universe will bring it to you. Don't think that just because you can't see every little movement, that it isn't being worked on because *it is being worked on and it is up to you to maintain the clear image of this.*

You will begin to build a new life and you will improve the conditions of your environment with new ideas. You will become aware of the way things *are* instead of being hindered by useless repetition of the way things appear. Your consciousness is enhanced and changed so that you begin to see the true world that lies hidden behind the veils of superficial appearances.

Your mental and physical body is made up of your perceptions and your belief systems. Your belief systems are what you believe in every area of your life. Your perceptions are what you have personally extrapolated from your experiences. Two people can see the same situation and both view it completely different. They have different perceptions. Why don't we all have the same perceptions? It is because you have been raised from a baby to adulthood within different environments, lifestyles, behaviors, likes and dislikes.

These are just a few circumstances that can alter your perceptions. You don't have to have the perceptions you do. They may simply have become comfortable over the years and you have just accepted that this is how it has to be. But it's not true. You can change any perception or belief you may currently have and replace it with a new one. At first your logical mind will put up a fuss and tell you this is ridiculous. It will tell you to be safe and keep thinking as you do. But how can you be safe and happy with the life you are leading right now minus any positive thoughts or things in your life?

Begin by throwing out those beliefs that no longer serve you and replace them with what you truly desire. And make sure to replace the negative thoughts and feelings with something positive. You can't take a belief that you have had for a very long time and then fail to replace it, because the old belief will come right back. Nature abhors a vacuum. Throw out all the perceptions that do not serve you well and build the new perceptions of what your life will be.

It is not wishing that makes something come to be, it is *believing* that something will come to be. A successful person believes in himself and pays little notice to mistakes, bad days, or setbacks. He focuses on his goal, knowing and believing that he will get there. He doesn't just wish he will get there, he *believes* he will get there. He feels and believes it and that is the kind of positive thought that will get you the life that you desire.

CHAPTER TWO

What Has Fear Ever Done for You?

Fear is the Thief of Dreams . . .

Fear is a feeling of lack of control over your world and everything in it. Control is a feeling of wanting to predict exactly what is going to happen. The trouble with both of these feelings is that they cause unstable, strong emotions that can wreak havoc with your positive thoughts.

Each has to do with fretting about what you feel and think can't be controlled. You want to control your world and you don't trust the Universe to control your world because if you did, you wouldn't feel the need to be controlling or fearful. Fear only lives when you don't understand that you are capable of having the power to create thought forms that the Universe will respond to.

Fear scares desire so you must get rid of fear. And when you look fear in the eye and realize that you can throw fear out the door, things begin to straighten out.

What does fear do for you?

Fear only brings you more to fear and it conveniently arrives through the thoughts and focuses of fear. Nothing is worth fearing. By focusing on a solution to the fear you will be in a positive frame of mind and things will change for the good.

You do not have to live in fear.

Haste Breeds Fear . . .

Whenever you are in a hurry, it is usually because you are afraid that you may be left behind, and if you are left behind, there are consequences to being left. If you hurry to an appointment you're in fear of the repercussions of not being on time.

Whether you are continually and unconsciously rushing everywhere, you are training your mind to be in some kind of fear. Your mind goes into an automatic thought process of fear and before you know it you are feeling more and more anxious. Soon things begin to keep happening that make you feel even more fearful and anxious.

But this can be easily changed through positive thought. Make the choice to weed out fear and replace it with ease and calm thoughts. Fear is a repetitive habit of the mind that is spawned directly from negative thoughts, through various environmental factors, and by self perception. You can be free of it, however, through action efforts and determination.

Fear as a Magnet? . . .

Strong expectation is a powerful magnet. If you have a strong and confident desire, the Universe will attract to you the things that will aid you... circumstances, people, and things as long as you desire with trust, confidence, calm and hope. But the same is true for if you fear a particular thing. The Universe will attract what you fear most if you focus on it long enough. This may be hard to swallow; in fact, it may even seem unfair. But the person who fears really expects whatever is feared will be delivered, just as easily as the one who attracts positivity. The choice is yours. Remember that in the eyes of the Universe it is all the same; the Universe is in the business of delivering what you want and desire, so if you crave fear that is what you will attract.

Trying to deny fear in your life is not going to help, but stating and feeling the opposite will. The best and easiest way is to see the life of positive thought that is the opposite of fear, constantly dwelling on the positive thoughts, and manifesting it into physical reality.

So instead of saying, *I'm not afraid* say strongly, *I am courageous.* To overcome fear, you will want to hang on tightly to the mental thoughts and feelings of courage. You want to say courage, act courageous, and think courageously. Keep a positive mental image of courage so that it becomes your primary repetitive thought pattern.

See the word *courage* sinking deeper into your mind and hold it strong there until the mind has permanently glued it in place. The mind will reject an initial original thought if it doesn't understand it or if it isn't within the established patterns of your personal being. But once you begin to get it used to the new way of thinking and retrain your new thought patterns it will become easier and easier.

Whenever fear arrives remember that fear paralyzes effort, and courage encourages activity. What do you prefer? A paralyzed effort, or positive movement? Fear is the parent of hate, jealousy, anger, discontent, failure, and we're sure you can think of a few more. If you can rid yourself of fear, you will rid yourself of fear's children as well. In order to be free, you have to get rid of the fear.

Ridding yourself of fear should be your first major step in applying the power of positive thought. Life will feel freer, happier, stronger, and more successful concerning everything in your life. Do your best to stop feeding the fear and its offspring. It may seem difficult at first but starve the fear to death, don't feed it.

Instead, start feeding your mind with positive, strong, fearless thoughts. Keep yourself busy by always thinking in fearlessness and the fear will die. Fearlessness is positive and fear is negative and the positive always wins. It's time to train your mind into new habits of thought. Kick out the old and bring in the new, and always remember that fear is the ultimate four-letter word.

CHAPTER THREE

Don't Worry? *How?!*

Pulling the Mental Weeds

It sounds so easy to just say, "Don't worry!" when you have so much to fear and worry about. What could possibly happen if you didn't worry? Would others look at you with scorn and say, *why isn't she worried? There is so much to anticipate and be afraid of!* What's someone to do when he thinks of all the possible things that are ahead that might upset him, or his plans? He is creating a world of worry for himself.

Most of the things that we fear never come true and if they do they arrive in a much milder form than was anticipated. And the majority of what you are afraid of never appears at all. Why waste time worrying about what might be when you can create with your own positive thoughts what *is* to be? Isn't it better to train your own mind to focus on the positive and separate yourself from worry?

How about concentrating on a solution while seeing life as easy as you want it to be? This will go far towards creating the life of your dreams. It's not that you have to actually fight worry because that is not how you rid yourself of worrisome thoughts anyway. Practice shifting your focus and concentrating on something in your life that is positive right now and the worry will disappear. The mind thinks of one thing at a time and focusing on a positive thought will replace any thoughts of worry.

When you hold on to thoughts of worry your mind can't find the time to work out the best plans that will benefit you. But when you focus on helpful and solution-oriented thoughts your subconscious will begin to work out how to bring those about for you. You will then start finding myriad methods that will help you achieve those thoughts.

Positive thoughts drive the worrisome thoughts away. Begin by finding the right positive attitude and you will find that all the rest will just fall into place.

Negative Emotions Breed Worry and Fear . . .

Every time you give in to negative emotions it makes it easier for the negative to bounce back. When you continually repeat a negative thought and/or emotion the subconscious takes over and begins unconscious repetition. As you embrace the negativity you begin to grow a fine garden of negative mental weeds.

Spaced among your lovely flowers of positive emotions and thoughts, you begin to litter your mental garden with weeds with each negative thought. Start pulling out those weeds by shifting focus to the positive in your life. Find the positive. Look for the positive. It is there! As you make an effort to grow a beautiful garden you will find it can happen as long as you keep up the weeding and replacing the negative seeds with beautiful, positive ones.

When you dwell on what you believe are the faults within yourself, you will attract that kind of thought current and actually increase the awareness of the faults you already think you possess. Think instead within the thought current of courage and of being deserving. Think of the good qualities you would like to possess. Imagine those qualities within yourself and make them a part of you. The more you can immerse yourself in the thought vibrations of what you truly want to be, the more you will draw out those qualities.

Know that the intensity and power of your focus will bring the desired results that you want. You will slowly rid yourself of fear as the power of positive thinking proves itself to you over and over again. You'll begin to see how the infinite energy will always care for you and take care *of* you if you allow it.

When you aim your mind in a certain direction all the things that you have wanted will begin coming to you with very little effort. Don't give any thought to possible obstacles or imagined disasters. Don't speak of yourself or anything that you do in a disapproving or self deprecating manner. Don't speak of times being hard. Create what you want. You are above fear. Fear and worry have no power unless you feed it power through your thoughts.

When others are having a hard time it does not mean that you will too. You will find great opportunity as you continue to keep yourself focused on the positive. Remember, thought vibrations are just as real as air and water. What you think and talk about will attract to you.

Counteract Worry with Good Vibrations . . .

If you could visibly see thought patterns you would see the myriad vibrations flowing to and from others.

You would see the people that have similar vibrations directly interacting through these vibrations while being drawn to one another. You would see someone that is angry displaying the same type of vibration as the person who they are interacting with. All the vibrations of a similar nature would be connecting each person through their thoughts and emotions.

Sometimes when people get together they gossip about others and they perhaps do not realize that they are drawing the mean gossip right back to them; the more minds that get together for a purpose, the stronger the vibrational current. Complainers and gossipers draw more complaints and gossip back to themselves. If you are always talking or thinking about what you believe are the shortcomings and imperfections in someone else you are only drawing back to yourself similar thoughts, actions, and experiences.

So how about using the power of thought for positive means, especially to counteract worry? If two people met each day and talked of great things and focused on the positive in others around them, they would attract such a beautiful life. If you spoke without controversy and did this with genuine emotion you could build anything that your heart desired.

And besides exhibiting caution with fear, worry, and control, there is another emotion that seems to get in the way of us obtaining our desires, and that would be impatience.

Impatience creates impatience and impatience is really just another form of worry. How about we exchange impatience for excited expectation instead? Being excited about something is great, but when we seem to think it is taking too long to arrive (by our calendars), the excitement turns into impatience. So do your best to change that impatience to excited expectation and let the Universe do its job.

Temporary Conditions . . .

When you change the rate of vibration, you change the quality, form, and nature of the object. We can change the vibration and produce any conditions that we desire to manifest. When our thoughts are filled with positive thoughts, we have moved vibrations in motion to bring us particular results.

When we change our vibration to negative thoughts we have set our vibrations in motions to bring us negative results. But remember that any negative condition — as well as positive — are temporary conditions and can be changed by your thoughts and feelings alone.

It's amazing how certain circumstances can change the body. When someone says something funny, your body shakes and you laugh which shows that thought has control over your muscles; or, when you hear something tenderly said, your eyes fill with tears which shows that it is thought and feeling that controls your glands in your body. These conditions are temporary, but the body within the subconscious mind reacts to thought. Let's think about this. Let's say you cut yourself. The subconscious mind sends thousands of cells to start healing at once and in a few days, your cut is healed.

Think about when you break a bone. Once the doctor has set it, it heals on its own because of the subconscious mind. If the doctor didn't set it, the subconscious would get to work to try to figure out how to heal it. We just take for granted the way our body works and how it works. Your automatic subconscious mind is responsible for that.

You can change its pattern and you can change your health or your weight or anything else for that matter. All these developments of the subconscious mind proceed without our personal direction and as long as we don't interfere, the result works out.

But these millions and millions of cells are all smart and they do respond to thought, and they can be slowed down or even be stopped by our thoughts of doubt, anxiety, or fear. They are like a group ready to start an important task but every time they embark on the plan, the plans change until they finally get discouraged and give up.

Every element of the human body is about the rate of vibration. We know that a higher rate of vibration controls, changes, and eliminates a lower rate of vibration. So how do you raise your vibrations? By visualizing and raising quite some time for your desires.

Many people begin focusing on what they want, and then they begin to worry because they didn't include some forgotten details. Just put the details in and that is all there is to it. Over thinking and micro managing will only cause worry and frustration. Keep your eyes on your desires and don't be concerned about how they will arrive. No micro managing required; only your vibrations through joyous thought.

If you want something you visualize and hold the mental image of it in the most positive and certain thought you can find within yourself. After you form the image you must be vigilant in having unquestioning faith that it is coming to you.

Don't speak of any other way than it coming to you. Say it as if it is already yours. It will be brought to you through your own feelings and thoughts of certainty. The Universe will begin to move energy and vibrations to match what you are wanting. When you focus with certainty you will have what you want as long as you don't throw any wrenches into the mix of doubt, worry, lack, or fear.

You can't possibly know what the Universe moves to help you get what you focus on. If you live in one part of the country, the Universe may bring a phone call from another part of the country to help hook you into the vibrations you are matching. That phone call could be part of what you are focusing on.

The Universe can bring so many things your way when you don't hang on to how you think it is going to happen. When you focus and visualize and keep strong in your positive thoughts and then let it go to the Universe, this frees the Universe in finding all kinds of ways to bring it to you. When you control how it happens, you will most likely be waiting for. So why worry? Like the man said... Don't worry, be happy!

The Opinions of Others . . .

The opinions of others can instigate worry and negatively affect your success. Many people are actually co-dependent on the opinions of others and while there never seems to be a shortage of opinions, it turns out that a large part of the roadblock to intentionally creating your world lies in these opinions of others.

There is nothing wrong with taking someone's advice if you feel it is something that is right. But to listen to dozens of unsolicited opinions of how to live life — that life being yours — seems not only counter productive; it means that someone else is trying to create your world.

When you accept the opinions of others as the truth, then their opinion morphs into the truth of your creation. Is that what you want? Think clearly when someone is offering you their opinion. If it is something that is going to affect your creation on any level, then you don't need it.

Here's an example: Some well meaning friend takes you to lunch. All through lunch she is telling you that you look great. She lets you know that if you lost a few pounds, then you would be a perfect woman. Now, is this opinion valid? Does it make you feel bad about yourself, or do you dwell on the fact that she thinks you look great? Do you even pay attention to what she is saying? This opinion is received with quietly hurt feelings. But what about the fact that you can either choose to accept what someone tells you or not? Again, if you accept their opinion, then that opinion becomes your truth so think carefully before you allow another's opinion into your world.

But how do you handle an opinion that is hurtful? You must first realize that the other person is feeling insecure inside since they obviously feel the need to invite someone else to the insecurity party. Remain balanced and let the unwanted (and unimportant) opinion slide off your back. You don't need unsolicited opinions and you can feel free to calmly keep them out of your world.

An aware human being knows that his activities, at all times, are in harmony. By staying balanced and in harmony you are free from the ups and downs of anything others say or do. Do your best to get rid of fear, anxiety, and the feelings of being rushed. Keep yourself balanced so you don't get into a negative space.

Get yourself used to — and expectant of — the feelings surrounding change.

Change is a good thing.

Change is forward movement.

Inform your mind that for every door that closes, a thousand more open. If change makes you uncomfortable, tell yourself that the change that you are experiencing is opening so many wonderful doors; portals to whatever you desire. Tell your survival self — that pesky, negative, unconscious self — to quiet down, because change is good. Oh, and DON'T WORRY!

CHAPTER FOUR

Thought is Motion

Using Mental Training . . .

Thought is motion. It is carried by vibrations similar to electricity and is given vitality by your emotions. The thought then takes form and expresses itself. In order to express purpose, the emotions have to be called on to give feeling to the thought so it will take form. How can we make sure this happens? By using mental training. It can be difficult but it gets easier each time, until it becomes automatic.

And what happens when you get the thought process into an automatic state? The automatic subconscious takes over. It starts a kind of recording loop and once this happens, your desire is there in the forefront.

The Universe, connected to the subconscious, begins changing, altering, and arranging all of the elements so that the closest equal to what you've been thinking is then manifested. The real substance of the physical world from which *all* forms detectable to human senses are built is mental energy (or thoughts) working at the subconscious level.

You create the thought through the conscious self and if you think about it over and over again, the subconscious takes over and places it on automatic, which in turn repeatedly creates the image adding feelings to the mix, then the Universe takes the image and gives back to you exactly what you have been thinking and feeling. So what is the best way to enter into the subconscious self? Through the conscious self.

The conscious self is the part of you that experiences physical life here on Earth. The spirit self is the part you can listen to (if you can hear it) that is a direct connection to the Universe and helps you move on a particular desire. You cannot predict the outcome of even the smallest act, and you do not know all the workings of all the forces that have been set in motion on your behalf.

Much might depend on you doing some small act. The small act could be the very thing that opens the door of opportunity to big possibilities. You can't possibly know all the combinations that the Universe is making for you in the physical world. So if you ignore doing some little thing it may cause a holdup getting what you want. Be aware of what should be acted upon once you start the process of intentional creation.

You don't have to remain on constant high alert or be concerned that you might miss the opportunity; if an opportunity passes there will be another one. You just want to be aware of when to act upon any opportunity that the Universe offers because you never know what it might lead to.

So how do your thoughts bring unwanted circumstances? By thinking, talking about, and visualizing circumstances of limitation, disease, lack, and conflict of every kind. These kinds of thoughts are grasped by the subconscious and the Universe inevitably brings these into physical form.

Taking Hold of Your Life

Your mental images that you have repetitively held in the past have created your present experiences. The state of today is always the result of the images you thought of in the past. Every thought we have brings movement — either negative or positive — to our physical selves as well as to elements of the brain. This actually sparks a physical change within the construct of our tissues, so this means that when we have a certain amount of repetitive thought patterns on any particular subject, these thoughts will spring to life based on what we continually focus on. Pretty powerful stuff!

As you send those images, thoughts, and feelings out to the Universe, it will respond by matching your vibration and send back to you exactly — or even a higher developed version of — what you emitted.

Every person has the power to generate what he or she wants. But most people tend to limit their thoughts to what others think. Look beyond mere appearances and see through your *own* perceptions, not the common ones held by most people. This is an important concept. Remember, truth becomes truth when a certain amount of people decide to perceive something in unison, and it then becomes their truth simply because they choose to believe it.

People begin to tell others that *this is so* and then find more recruits to agree with their collective point of view. This is how something becomes truth. If you have any doubts about this, consider the Flat Earth Society. How many hundreds if not thousands of years did mankind believe the world was flat? To these learned scholars, and all who were under their tutelage, the world was flat. That was the truth of the time.

By not accepting at face value the common perceptions that most people carry, and by finding out what your own truth is, happiness and success will be that much closer to you. The question to ask yourself is do you in fact currently believe what *you* want to believe? Or have you simply adopted your beliefs from your family and friends or even from a well meaning teacher? When you find the true core of you — the truth that you want to live — you will be in the alignment necessary to obtaining what you desire in life.

Every one of us lives in a world of our own creation. You have constructed your creation according to your own mental repetitive patterns. If you change the pattern, you will change your world. So if your world currently isn't what you like, you have the power to change it. You don't need lessons on how to 'get' power, because you already possess the power to make your life the way that you want.

Take responsibility — it's different from blame — that you created every facet of your life. It can be difficult to understand why we would create a world of lack for ourselves and it was likely unintentional, but now that you know that you can intentionally create your world, take responsibility for your thoughts and feelings and realize that you have the power. You were given this power at birth and it is meant to be used by you.

When you are determined to do something and stick to it, you emit mental patterns that put you in touch with other like-minded people who will directly or indirectly bring you the materials you need for the completion of your plans. Be responsible with your thoughts and feelings. Remove from your consciousness all thoughts of the future. You are making a mental picture which actually exists in the *now*.

Keep the idea of your purpose and all that you want out of life in the *now*. When you know, even when your eyes tell you differently, that everything is instantly okay at all times, *it is*. Living in the now, not in the past or the future, will ensure that you get what you want in life. Visualizing and creating what you want right now and playing it in your mind each day will bring it to you.

Focus on the future and your desires will remain in the future but by focusing on the joy of the day and imagining the life that you want 'in the now' the Universe will bring it to you. If you don't have the funds to live the life you want just yet live it within your own mind at first. Start there and as each day goes by and as you build those intense thoughts and positive feelings you will manifest your life's desires.

Successful people live unconsciously with this law. Their wisdom within tells them to get into the thought processes of the successful mind and that is what they attract. Think about what you can do by focusing on, talking about, and visualizing circumstances of unlimited possibilities; perfect health, abundance, and resolutions of every kind.

These kinds of thoughts are *also* just as easily taken up by the subconscious and the Universe inevitably brings them into physical form as well. Which do you choose?

There is just one sense, the sense of feeling, and all the other senses are really variations of this. This is why emotions prevail so readily over the mind and why we have to emit feelings hand in hand with thought if we want positive results.

Thoughts coupled with feelings are the perfect blend. We are used to looking at the world with our five senses and from these experiences our perceptions are born. But true perceptions are only found from within the spirit self or your insight, which requires an increase in the vibrations of the mind and can only manifest when the mind is concentrated in a certain direction.

Repetitive concentration means you should have an even, unbroken flow of thought for a length of time everyday if you want to focus on attaining your desires.

How do you know this will work? By knowing that your spirit self is always connected to the Universe.

Why worry or fear that your purpose won't come to you? You know exactly what you want and you are always connected to the Universe. So as long as you use the Universal Laws correctly, you will attract and have what you want.

You must trust the Universe. You must trust yourself. And you must trust that any and every thing that you see — even if you perceive that it is a difficult situation — is working toward your desire. When you trust the Universe and do your part by visualizing and focusing on what you want, you will have it.

Your life from this day forward should be what you want it to be. No more days of worry, no more allowing others' opinions unduly influence you, and no more thoughts of lack because when you know that the Universe is taking care of you, and when you believe it, the Universe acts on that.

That is not to say that the Universe wouldn't take care of you if you didn't believe in any, some, or most of the Laws of the Universe but you are the one responsible — based upon your perceptions — for attracting what you focus on. The Universe just acts upon your thoughts. The Universe is always there, whatever situation you have created, but by *consciously* creating your world you can have it all. The practice of focus requires being in charge of your mental and physical states and doing your best to keep the mind and body from wandering off during your visualization sessions, as well as during daily life. We often talk about how when you try to focus during quiet time, that the mind 'chatters'. This isn't the only time the mind chatters. You have mind chatter whenever you are engaged in worry or fear. This monkey chatter creates thoughts that expand your negative outlook so it's important to be aware of the chatter in order to slow it down. It's not possible to stop it completely, but it *is* possible to calm the chatter.

Meditation techniques and learning to take charge and being aware of what your little mind monkeys are doing can help stem the tide. By knowing that your little mind monkeys are acting up again, you will know how to calm them.

Insight . . .

Get used to trusting your own insight. Insight finds answers without the assistance of experience or memory.

Insight solves problems that are outside the scope of reason. Insight usually arrives so suddenly that it can sometimes be astonishing. It can suddenly shed light on something that we have been searching for — so directly that it seems that the answer must have come directly from the higher power.

Insight *can* be developed. If you want to develop your insight you want to first be able to recognize and appreciate it.

If you have an insightful moment, know that insight usually arrives in silence during times of quiet and calm. This is where you will discover *your* finest thoughts; thoughts that will ultimately lead you to your treasure.

There Really are No Limits . . .

You and the Universe are a team. Your wants, your thoughts, and your beliefs need to be in alignment. If one part of you doesn't support your intention, it will sabotage you. When it is not going as you want it to, that means some part of you doesn't want it. By changing your beliefs to fit your intention you will heal the sabotaging part of you and everything will begin to run effortlessly.

Keep your energy flow balanced.

When you 'push against' something you don't want, you are just about guaranteed it will come straight to you. When you push too hard with any desire, it's like taking a square peg and trying to push it through a round hole. Remember... *with ease.* Everything you do, *do with ease.* If you have to push then you are not letting the Universe take care of it. What is your part of the job? Visualizing and feeling good about your intention. That is it. The Universe takes care of the rest.

Always visualize with a clear image and a positive feeling. If you are not in the mood to visualize, *don't do it* because any negative feelings generated will taint your intention and while you may obtain a facsimile of your desire, it will possibly be a distorted version of what you originally wanted.

However, if your thought-intention is created in harmony with the Universe, it will arrive in a harmonic condition. Conversely, thought that is destructive will produce destructive results. The Universe is unconditional so the more aware you are that you are one with the Universe, the less aware you will be of circumstances and limitations.

When you have realized that you can create anything — and truly trust and believe that — then you are free of any conditions or limitations. Anything, *and we mean anything,* which you hold in your consciousness will become a pattern that will manifest physically in your life.

Is it easy to change the mental patterns? Not always, but with persistence it can be accomplished. These are mental images that have been photographed on the brain. So if you don't like the pictures, get rid of the negatives and create new photos through your visualization.

There is no limit when it comes to what you are thinking and there is no limit to the things that you can draw to yourself through thought. The physical supply on this earth is inexhaustible and the invisible supply of thought is inexhaustible. You can believe that you will have a million dollars and it will come to you, as long as you believe in that. If you feel and think it isn't possible to draw this to yourself, you won't be able to draw this into your life no matter what you do.

It is always about your thoughts and beliefs and the limits that you impose upon your thinking that determines what your life will become. As we discussed previously, everything in the world is made of the same substance, the same energy. New shapes and forms are constantly being made while older ones just dissolve away but all is made from the same energy.

And it's good to know that there is no limit to the supply of energy available to make whatever you want in life. Nature provides an unlimited and inexhaustible supply of riches and the supply never dwindles. The substance of the Universe will respond to your needs, it will not let the world go without any good thing.

The energy substance is very intelligent; it thinks, and it is alive and always wants more life in everything it surrounds. It wants consciousness to seek out how to extend the boundaries and find even a more complete expression through life. The Universe is a living presence that keeps creating and keeps thinking, just as we do. And we are the sparks off the Universe creating just as it intended for us to do.

Abundance ...

Never stop at the obviously visible supply. This is limiting. Always look to the limitless riches of the Universe and know that these come to you as fast you can receive and use them. You don't need to worry about losing what you want, fearful that someone else might beat you to it. It can't happen. There is an unlimited supply of everything that you want. You will always get what you focus on *or better.* And whatever is better is provided by the Universe which knows every little vibration that you emit.

It's not possible to see a true picture of wealth if you constantly look at wealth's opposite. Talking about the past troubles of your finances will bring you more of that past that upset you in the first place.

You don't have to think of this. Examine why whatever it is may have happened and then move on and forget about it. Don't rehash the hardships of the past generations of your family as these memories also bring you more of what you don't want. Instead, focus on the joyful family stories that build wonderful energy for your present life.

Acknowledge how a past ancestor overcame their hardship, but don't focus on the hardship itself. When focusing on the hard times you will begin to move things in your own life in that direction.

Accept that the Universe wants you to have happiness and know it can be in your life at all times. Talking about or reading conflicting theories of what you believe will only bring you more conflict. Listening to and reading pessimistic works that promote negative thoughts will only bring you more of these.

Choose to focus on works that make you feel good and help support what you believe is the truth. No matter how bad things can seem in your life or in the lives of others, you are just wasting your energy by focusing on the worry and negativity in the situation.

Start to envision yourself and the world becoming wealthy.

Focus on the abundance in the world instead of the lack. This will help you as well as everyone else who also elects to shift focus. And eventually you will begin to see more positive than negative everywhere around you.

Food for Thought . . .

When you get into positive thought vibration you may find that for a short while you experience more uneasiness than you ever have. The new change detects all the little negative thoughts you were having and begins to repel them. This may in turn cause a struggle, as your physical self (for a short time) will be affected by this.

It's like cleaning your house and the dust gets stirred up. But after the dusting, think how wonderful it feels to have a nice clean home. This is what it is like when you begin changing your patterns.

Concentration ...

When you practice concentration you are working with a *real* force of energy. Here is an example to help you understand the power of concentration.

Let's imagine that the Sun is the Universe, and your thoughts are the magnifying glass.

When you hold a magnifying glass in which the rays of the Sun are focused and you move the magnifying glass around, nothing happens. But let's say you take your magnifying glass and hold it still, focusing it on a single blade of grass. We know what happens from there. So imagine that the blade of grass is your desire and by focusing your magnifying glass on that one blade of grass the Sun will do what it does. Creating with the Universe is just like this example.

Attention vs. Concentration ...

But remember, attention is different than concentration. You do not concentrate attention. Attention is the means that helps you to concentrate mental force. The result is that you intensify energy so that you may direct it usefully.

Why is having a clear accurate image so necessary? Because 'seeing' creates the feeling and feeling creates the fruition of the desire.

First comes the mental (seeing) then the emotional (feeling) then the unlimited possibilities of creation (fruition).

Here is an amazing key to getting that clear image to stick. Take your clear image and imagine that you are printing this image on the cells of your brain *at the back of your head*. Carry the picture mentally to the back of your brain and see yourself keeping it there.

The sight center, for seeing what you see with your eyes, is located at the back of your head and the cells of that center are the ones that provide you with all of your visual images. When light hits your retina, an actual chemical reaction occurs that carries the image back to the cells of the sight center, where they go into action giving you the ability to see and an extrasensory link of the image enters into your consciousness.

When you send the image to the back of your head, you perform the act of 'seeing'. You are in fact taking the actual image and imprinting it into your psyche. When you do this repeatedly it becomes so.

Visualizing is the practice of creating mind images. The images are the mold which represents the pattern of your future. Make your pattern as clear as possible and while you're at it, make it wonderful. Don't be afraid to create it just as you please. There are no limitations to be placed upon you by anyone except yourself.

Constant Gardening . . .

When you plant a garden, you know what your harvest will be based on the seeds you planted. And you know what to do to make your garden grow.

Using positive thought and the Law of Attraction, the Universe takes care of how events will unfold as long as you tend your seed. You plan when and where the seed will be placed in the garden and the Universe takes care of the growth.

When you build a home, you make a plan describing where the kitchen will be, where the rooms will be, and what your yard will look like. Then you hand it over to someone who knows how to build the home based on your plans. The plan might be a little unfocused at first but then it will start to take shape, and what was once just an outline will begin to take form.

When you create images like this in your mind, clear and exact, it is much easier for the Universe to fulfill your desires. The Universe doesn't have to close any gaps caused by an unfocused desire. Get that clear image in your mind and the Universe will take care of the rest. And you have over four million workers on your side called brain cells!

In time you will receive signs from the Universe directing the best course of action for you at the right time and in the right way. Sincere desire will bring you positive belief and this will in turn provide the faith to know that your desire is truly yours.

Feeling gives the thought life and the will holds onto it firmly until the Universe brings it into manifestation. Give no thought to your external world right now. Make the world that you are creating wonderful and full of your desires.

CHAPTER FIVE

Affirmations

Say What You Want and Get It . . .

Affirmations are a huge part of changing your mental patterns to positive thought. Affirmations can create new mental attitudes within you and can help in the direction of making ourselves over.

They also raise the mental vibration so we can benefit from what comes with positive vibrations. Whether you know it or not, you are making affirmations all day long, unintentionally or intentionally. The person who says, "I can do it no matter what," is making an affirmation.

Did You Say Fail?

You also might be thinking to yourself that you have failed in the past and will always be a failure. Watch it, because assumption of failure can be a very powerful affirmation in its own right.

When you concentrate on being a failure you will certainly become one. But before you metaphorically throw yourself under the bus, remember that anything you have done in life — any experience you had — you thought was the right direction for you to pursue at the time.

The person who says, "I am doomed to fail," is making an affirmation. Each one starts the mental vibrations. So it's best to not be affected by the negative affirmations you might create, or of those around you. Rise up and stay within a positive affirmation zone and you will not be affected by the negative affirmations of others.

You will become immune to their rants of negativity if you remain in positive thought. Find yourself positive affirmations and begin to recite three or four of them a day for a week. Then the next week, change them out for some others.

Making and keeping track of your positive affirmations throughout the day create even stronger positive vibrations. Find the kind of affirmations that work for you and implement them right away.

Use Your Will . . .

You will have to use your own will to keep yourself thinking and acting in a positive manner. Don't try to send your thoughts to act on things or people. Keep your thoughts at home because you can accomplish much more.

Use your mind to make an image of what you want to have in your life and hold the focus with complete trust and faith. Use your will to keep your mind working in the direction of your focus. When you are out and about and you have a moment of negative persuasion about your life you are creating, gently move your mind back to the focus of what you want and keep in a positive space.

The more you keep continuous faith and trust in yourself and the Universe the more quickly will have what it is that you want. Positive images, thoughts, and feelings will begin emitting out from you and this energy will come back to you in some shape or form through the Universe. Things begin to move into motion to give you what you focus on. Every living and non living thing that is not yet created begins to move toward bringing into being what you want.

Every moment that you spend doubting, worrying, and fearing is a moment that you spend in disbelief. This sends the vibration of energy in a different direction than when you are thinking in positive thought. This is when your will is so important. It is your will that will determine what things you decide to give your attention to. If you want to become abundant it is important not to sit and study how to be poor through your own thoughts. Things are not brought about by thinking about their opposites.

Use your will to focus on abundance, good health, a wonderful career, and a pleasing relationship. Don't waste your time on thinking of the lack of what you feel you don't have. Begin to focus on what you desire and visualize it happening at this very moment and those moments will create your future.

And if something doesn't work out, consider what you learned from whatever the experience was and move on from it. *There is no failure.* Only decisions you made based on what you thought would likely occur. And you obviously had positive hope in the picture as well. You never set out to make a mess of things.

Now that you know that you can change your outcome by seeing whatever the event happens to be 'in your now', by changing your now into a positive experience it will become your future. Read the above paragraph until it fully connects with your consciousness. Do not move forward until you fully grasp the significance of it.

Then know that while you might expect something to come within a certain time frame and it doesn't, you should never think that this represents failure. Remember, thoughts of failure or other negative thoughts will become your affirmations if you let them. If you will instead hold on to your trust in the Universe and stop doubting your own ability to create what you want you will be on the road to success.

To Successfully Manage Your Affirmations . . .

- Don't gossip.

- Don't discuss the shortcomings of another individual.

- Try not to discuss any unlovable qualities or traits about another person, because you are hurting your own self when you do. Remember that by doing this you are attracting whatever you think and feel, so why invite bad feelings? Remember that the mental focuses enjoy just as definite a reality as anything physical.

- Don't compete. We're not talking about games of competition; we're talking about competing with another's life. You are here to create, not to compete for what you have already created.

- You don't have to take anything away from anyone and you don't have to cheat or take advantage of anyone. The Universe is unlimited. There is enough for everyone.

- Don't tell others of your past failures or financial troubles. Don't think of them at all.

- Don't talk to others about the hardships or poverty within generations of your family. Whenever you do this you mentally place yourself in a 'materially poor' category and this attracts the 'poor life' towards you.

- Don't brag or boast. When you find a boastful person, you find someone who is secretly fearful and doubtful. By just knowing that your desires are being met and that you see them met, people will become attracted to your success.

- Guard your speech. Don't speak of yourself, your life, or of anything else in a negative way. Even if you see an obstacle, remember that through the Law of Attraction when one door closes, thousands open.

Personal Action . . .

Thinking certain thoughts will bring you the life you desire but don't just use thought alone. You want to pay attention to action that you want to take as well. Where many people applying thought run into problems is by not connecting their thoughts to their personal action.

You must not only think but also show the Universe you mean it with personal action. Your thoughts — affirmations, really — make all things work to bring you what you want but your personal action must be that you are ready to receive when what you want reaches you. Begin imagining and affirming the opportunities that come your way to help you along. This is just the Universe answering your affirmations and bringing the vibrations of your wants to you. Use mental thought processes to get the ball rolling but also utilize the physical to begin to live it. If your want is to travel, pore over travel books to see what it will be like. See the signs that come your way to act upon getting your desire.

You don't want to give your image over to the Universe and just sit and wait for results. If you do, you won't get them. Act now because the only time there is 'is now'.

Prepare to receive what you want and do this by enjoying the process of your life while weeding out the negative affirmations of doubt, worry, and fear. Act upon the situations that come to you that you recognize are a part of your desire.

You can't act where you are not, you can't act where you have been, and you can't act where you are going to be. You can only act on where you are at the moment. Use that moment to live life as you want it to be, if only in your mind. This image will begin to merge with the life you are presently leading and your future will become the thoughts you generate today.

No worries if yesterday was negative, no worries if tomorrow will be negative, just live in the moment of today in positive thought. When you hold the vision of what you want and continue to have purpose in the life you are having now you will have what you want, not even a question.

Who Do You Want to Be?

Do you ever notice another person and wish you looked like them instead of you? Do you ever think or feel badly about your own self? If you don't love yourself, how is the Universe going to bring you what you desire when you may be expressing feelings that clearly don't match your desires? Be who you wish to be. Act as if you are already who you want to be.

If you see yourself a few pounds lighter, then see yourself that way. If you see yourself being more outgoing, take action and be a little more outgoing. If you can't quite get there yet, then dream about it in your head and think of the things you can do as the person you wish to be. Take some kind of action to let the Universe know you are serious. Let the Universe know that you are being who you want to be and the Universe will respond.

Some of us, when we look in the mirror, see all that is wrong. The funny thing is, there is no wrong. Take a look in the mirror. Really take a look in the mirror at the person you are. We are not talking about your outward appearance; we are talking about your inner being. You are just like us. We are just like you. Strip us of the physical, we are all alike and think and feel the same things. Your outward appearance is only your physical vehicle enabling you to create. If you have the ability to create anything in your life, don't you think you might also have the ability to create your physical appearance as well?

We heard the most wonderful line many years ago: Someone had asked a true master of life that if we can create anything why don't we have two extra arms to use? The master replied, "You could have the extra arms if you really believed you could."

Many people have a problem believing that they deserve all their wants. They self sabotage themselves because they don't believe they could possibly have everything they want. Every person on this earth has made mistakes.

We've all made mistakes, some of us small ones and some of us bigger. They're really not mistakes. They are decisions that were made from a perception of what you thought at the time and it just happened to have a result that you created. Let it go. The past is the past. Every human being on this earth deserves everything that they desire.

This bears repeating. Each one of us came from the same source and we all started out the same. If you strip us of this physical body, we are all the same. We have an eternal spirit. We all go back to the same source. Sure, we all make different decisions in creating our world but that is why we are here, to create. When we are done, we head back to the All and become one again.

So we all start out the same and we all go back the same. We all deserve everything that we desire. We are here to create and there is an unlimited supply. What you hold in your consciousness becomes. You can state the present reality of your mental patterns and they have real substance. They can be solidified into physical manifestation.

Picture the state of complete harmony in every area of your life. Trust the Universe to bring your exact images to you. The Universe has been bringing you what you have been focusing on all your life and now that you know, use the power of positive thought intentionally.

Here is Food for Thought . . .

Do you know that every time you are thankful for something, every time that you feel joyous about something, every time you admire something, you are telling the

Universe, *I want more of this!* And what does the Universe do the more you say you want more of that? It brings it to you!

It is not your job to *make* anything happen.

It's your job to envision it, and let it happen. In your happiness, you create something and then you uphold your vibration in accord with it, and the Universe will find a way to bring it to you. The growing spirit must realize that it has within itself all that is required. It can gladly accept from others suggestions, bits of knowledge, and advice. And the spirit itself is the only judge of what it requires at that moment. But it all comes down to you.

All the teachings in the Universe won't help you unless you take hold of the matter yourself and work it all out in your truth. You must apply and practice. The real work must be done by you.

Remember These Words . . .

Find the stillness. You know, the time when you sit and visualize or you sit and reflect. That stillness is merely *you* connecting with the *original you;* the "you" that has always been, the "you" that was you before coming into this world. You are inside of your physical vehicle. You observe from your consciousness.

Your consciousness is you, not your physical body.

Your physical body is a means to observe and create for your consciousness. When someone asks *Who are you?* you may give the label of your name, but you were consciousness before you were labeled. Your spirit self is you and always will be; even when your physical body isn't around anymore. But you will still live.

It's important to know this and see that things are just "things" and that we are always alive and our spirits never tire. It's our physical being that can tire. By knowing this, we can see that we are merely observing through a physical body and that we are always all right. Our spirit doesn't get ill, our spirit never tires, our spirit doesn't even need to eat; we are everything that we should be from spirit perspective.

We are merely living on this physical earth in order to understand what it is like to create and to love. When we come from a place where we knew nothing but love, we had nothing to compare it to; no contrast. We wanted to experience contrast and learn to create, and we were given that choice so here we are... but we never leave from our original consciousness. We are always okay. At all times.

Find the stillness, the spirit self, your consciousness, and acknowledge it by saying an inward hello. That stillness is really you. The body you have isn't really you, just a vehicle for living on Earth. If you connect with the stillness, you will always be fine. If you are angry, just find the stillness. The stillness doesn't become angry, only the physical vehicle so find the stillness to dissipate the anger.

Some Affirmative Thoughts . . .

If you want to rid yourself of something, whether it is fear, lack, or disease, think upon the exact opposite. If you want to rid yourself of lack, think of abundance. If you want to rid yourself of disease, think of health. Keep your mind focused on the equal opposite of what you want to be rid of.

Disregard others' opinions about what you are doing with your life. Better yet, remain silent about the changes you are making. You are not creating alone. You and the Universe are a team. If you have a human co creator in your life tell them all that you are doing but if you are doing this on your own, be silent. There is power in silence. When you are building energy with your visualizations and you are getting more excited and joyous about your life becoming what you want it to be it becomes so. But sometimes when you tell someone about what you are doing and you get a disapproving look or comment, it could affect your outcome if you let it.

This dissipates the energy from your want when you have doubt from yourself or another. The other person's opinion does not matter unless you let it. Why even mess with it? Keep it to yourself and start enjoying life now. Get into the feeling of enjoying life and let the Universe bring you all you desire through your feelings and thoughts.

CHAPTER SIX

The Emotional Roller Coaster

Jealousy and Envy . . .

You come home from work and see that your next door neighbor, once again, has another new vehicle. You feel envious and wish it was you. *Why does he get everything?* you think to yourself. Or maybe your cousin calls to tell you she's getting married. Through clenched teeth you tell her how happy you are for her and when you hang up the phone, you turn into a green eyed monster chock-full of jealousy. You were supposed to get married before her!

Jealousy and envy land in the same family of feelings and they are both a negative emotion that will attract back to you faster than you can say, "I do!" They both possess intense emotions and the thoughts that run through someone's mind usually are repetitive.

We have negative and positive emotions for a reason. We don't ignore our less than positive emotions but we do learn how to balance the emotions so that we can use them constructively.

Between the intense emotion and the repetitive thoughts of jealousy or envy, you will have just moved your focus into supersonic speed and everyone around you will continue to make you jealous and envious until you carry out a thoughts and feelings check.

So how do you change this? You can change these intense emotions with just a few adjustments to your perception. Let's begin with envy.

When you see someone obtain what they want, instead of saying how much you wish you were that person or how much you want what they have, change your perceptions and thoughts to the positive, which will in turn get rid of the envy.

So your neighbors seem to have everything that it is that you want. Instead of wishing you were them, be grateful to the

Universe for giving you a sign that you are next in line for the new car. This could be an indicator from the Universe shown through your own neighbor.

Think how great it will be when it comes to you as well. Get away from being envious of the neighbor and turn your attention to thanking the Universe, trusting the Universe, and knowing that you will get just what you asked for as well.

Now let's tackle jealousy.

Jealousy is merely a form of insecurity in you. When you are jealous you want what someone else has with intensity that goes beyond envy. When jealousy rears its ugly head, you're mad because you deserve it more than him or her, and you have waited longer.

If you are applying the Law of Attraction and trusting the Universe doesn't this mean you will have what you want as well? You will receive it in the time that the Universe lines it all up for you.

You have to be in alignment with your desire for it to come to you. Just because one person has what you want doesn't mean that you won't get it as well. Who cares who gets it first? Don't worry about others and just focus on your own creation of your life.

The happier you are for the other person, the more aligned you will be for your own creation. The Universe is unlimited and has more resources than you can even imagine and is bringing you your desire as long as your thoughts and feelings match up to what you want. Others have their own lives to create.

There is no need to be jealous of another's creation. Remember that you can create just what they have if you wanted to or even better.

When One Door Closes . . .

When you are faced with a challenge in your life and it feels as if all the doors are closing, what do you do? Do you accept the fact that things seem to be falling apart or do you rise to the occasion and keep moving forward?

If you keep the focus on what you want, and a door closes, then this means that many more doors will soon open for you. If you are focusing on what you want with positive expectations and trust the Universe will help you with what avenues to take or not to take.

The Universe knows what is behind the closed door and it obviously knows that it wouldn't have worked out at the moment. Trust in the Universe and keep your eyes open for all the other opportunities that will be shown to you. You never know that the door that closed could reopen in a whole different way. The Universe knows what it is doing.

Trust the process. Trust in the Universe when something doesn't go 'just right'. The Universe has many ways to bring to you what you focus on through the Law of Attraction.

When you tell it which door you have to go through it can take a much longer time for something to manifest because of the limited path you have placed on the desire. Seeing only the end result of what you want and then giving it to the Universe to take care of the 'how' will bring you your desire much faster and possibly in a way that you have never even thought of.

Get into the habit of thinking positively when something doesn't go right. Realize that the Universe is helping to bring you what you have focused on. The Universe has cleared a particular path and knows the one that isn't the way to go. When one door closes, another door always opens.

Get into the mindset of remaining positive even during seemingly hard times. Those positive thoughts will be emitted and return to you exactly as you focused on or better.

Be open to the way things come to you and when a door seems to close, smile and realize the Universe has something much bigger and better in mind to bring to you.

Taking Care of the Inner You . . .

We remember the days when we were always trying to catch up, constantly feeling as if we were always chasing down our dreams and our lives. Time would seem to get away and we felt like we never had enough time to get it all done. This was before we found the knowledge of what life is really about, and when we finally did, things began to change.

You see, all the rushing around and trying to get it all done was attracting more of the same; the ever vigilant Law of Attraction was in motion as it always is.

We just weren't aware of it yet. When we became tired of the rat race and listening to others' opinions of what our lives should be, we went searching for the real answers. We knew there was more to life than working at a job we didn't want to be at, and a life full of chasing.

Over many years, finding and studying what we felt was our truth, we began to see that even though we are physical beings we are also a spiritual being and it was important to pay just as much attention to the inner self as we gave to physical outer self. When we're told to take care of ourselves we tend to focus on activities like exercise and eating right without giving a second thought to our inner selves.

We take for granted that we breathe in and breathe out without even thinking that maybe the inner self has functional requirements, too. Your physical being would not exist without that inner self that keeps in mind the journey you agreed to take before coming to this physical world. It keeps you focused on what you wanted to experience and grow through here on earth.

How it all comes about fits into the sphere of free will but the inner self has everything to do with what you do here. Your inner self should be taken care of at least as well as you take care of your physical body.

Your inner self needs nourishment or you are liable to become an unbalanced being which gives you a distinct disadvantage in creating the life you want through the Law of Attraction.

So how do you feed your soul? Many people feed it through religion and prayer and others through inspiration.

However you feed it is up to you. How you feed your spirit should feel joyful and refreshed after. If you don't, if how you feed your soul leaves you with feelings of doubt or fear, then you need to develop another way.

Meditation is a positive way to connect to the inner you, as well as visualization. This places you in a zone where anything is possible; and, you are then working with your logical mind as well as the spirit mind in order to manifest your wants.

It gives you a chance to step away from the current reality and instead create the reality you truly desire as long as you are passionate about what you focus on.

By feeding all aspects of yourself you will find that life will become more balanced, less hectic, and you will feel like you are moving forward instead of standing still.

You will find that fear and doubt leave your life as you connect with your inner you.

Change, the Best Indicator . . .

Most people are not comfortable with change. They prefer the predictable scenarios in life because they see this as calm and easy, but in order to make life better and get out the rut you may be in, change is an important indicator to show where your life is going. So how can change be a good thing in your life? Let's start at the beginning.

When you find the Law of Attraction and realize that it has been working in your life without you consciously knowing it, it seems like such a simple concept: Change your thoughts, change your life. Could it really be this easy? It really depends on how you look at it.

When you begin to apply the Law of Attraction intentionally you find that you have many negative thoughts that you didn't even know were there. You have a nice visualization and you're feeling 'the now' of the life you want and then some negative thoughts creep in telling you that it isn't possible — to think something into existence.

Whether you believe in the negative thought or not, it did creep in. It's what you do with the negative thought and it is how you ultimately change your way of thinking that will bring you the life you want, and doing both of these takes change on your part.

Figuring out what causes you to believe a certain way will help you to learn if the belief you have is serving you well. This belief could be from your own perception of life, or might have come from a family member whose habits and beliefs you may have picked up. But no matter what, you have to change it if it is not to your benefit or the life you envision. Change your beliefs to reflect what you want in life.

For example, let's say you have always believed that when you get older you get sick. This thought may have come from society or even your own family but it is now your belief. So if you are not comfortable with that thought, change it.

I believe that as I get older I will be healthy and joyful. That is all there is to it except that now you must adopt your new way of thinking as a core belief in your daily life. But what if you don't believe your new statement? You may want to start with a small step in order for the logical mind to grasp the concept and see it manifest, then you will become more confident in your manifesting ability and can then move on to a larger step.

What about those negative thoughts that creep up on you? You can't fake it and say, *This does not bother me,* and then fume inside. You have to inwardly release the negative thoughts or situations and keep your eyes fixed on the life you truly want. The less energy you pay to the negative the less negative you will experience. So it takes change from you once again.

Life will change. It can slowly change, quickly change, and change intermittently, depending on what feelings and thoughts you emit to the Universe. Sometimes others get upset because life goes topsy-turvy and it feels as if things are getting worse. Don't buy into it.

Keep your eyes on the life you want and realize your life will change to the life you desire. Sometimes there are 'clearing out' days that have to take place because this is one of the ways the Universe takes care of you, but as long as you trust and know that your vision is coming just live through the seemingly negative with ease. *Always with ease.*

Change is a wonderful indicator that the life you want is right here, now, and that the Universe is bringing it to you with all the bells and whistles intact. Be grateful to see this great indicator come into your life when using the Law of Attraction.

Strength of Belief . . .

Belief in what you desire is one of the most important thoughts and feelings when it comes to the Law of Attraction. We have all kinds of different beliefs. Your beliefs in the world and your own world make a huge difference in what will be attracted to you through the Law of Attraction.

Take a good look at what your beliefs are within your own mind. Do you believe that your desires will manifest? Do you believe that no matter what your circumstance that you can change the outcome with your thoughts and feelings?

Or do you have a belief that has been passed down from generation to generation that could be inhibiting your own thoughts about what life is all about? Start new with your beliefs.

Begin by thinking about what you truly believe. Do you have thoughts of lack when it comes to what you desire? These can be a generational thought pattern that you grew up with that can keep you from attaining the life that you want. Find the thoughts that could be keeping you from having full belief in the Law of Attraction and your life.

Sitting on the fence between two opposing beliefs can leave you... *sitting on the fence;* not making a decision either way about what you think can happen in your life. Neither belief is necessarily wrong but one will be responsible for the outcome that you want in your life while the other will be the one that keeps you stagnant in the life you are currently living.

So what if your beliefs are different than your family or your friends or even the rest of the world? Is that a problem for you? Do you feel the need to accept a belief so that others won't look at you and snicker because *you could be wrong?* Everyone has their own truth and each truth is just as real as the next. Live the truths and your beliefs how you want to live them, not dictated by others' opinions of what they feel is right for you.

All true and good beliefs lead back to the same form anyway, which is unconditional love and joy. If you are not feeling unconditional love from within, it is time to find the beliefs that will create those feelings for you.

The strength of your beliefs is what will propel you to what you want in life. Having said that, many believe that this is a just a form of denial; that the real world has all these struggles to contend with. *How can I possibly change things in my life with just a thought and a feeling?*

So what if you are denying what you don't want in your life. If focusing on what you want in this lifetime happens to be a problem for someone else so what? You can have it all. You can achieve what you want. There is no doubt about it. And we hope the image you have in your mind is the real truth for you.

Time Delay . . .

Why does it seem to take so long to manifest certain desires? Why is it so easy to manifest a parking spot or a penny on the sidewalk, but so difficult to manifest the beautiful home and the financial security you want? And is there always a time delay in manifesting and creating your desires into physical reality?

Some things do have a time delay involved when it comes to the Law of Attraction but there is a reason for it. Remember that when you focus on something and put energy into it the Universe is going to bring you either what you focused on, or better.

The Universe must be able to move mountains, situations, and people in order to bring you the objects of your focus. But it isn't only about your focus; it is about everyone who will be involved in helping you realize your creation, as well. The Universe is lining up and matching every vibration, something we call the universal dance.

The Universe is also building a solid foundation for your desires through your repetitive focus, thoughts, and emotions. Think of each thought, emotion, and focus as pieces of lumber. Each piece is another part of your desire; the more pieces, the more solid the foundation.

Now toss in a couple of pieces of lumber that are gnarled, old, and rotten. These represent your negative thoughts and emotions. If they are directed at your desire as a thought of lack, then you are taking an old piece of lumber and making it part of your desire, right along with all of the beautifully milled lumber.

Which pieces of lumber will build a house of desire, and which ones will be responsible for the lack of a solid foundation? This is what can cause a time delay as well. When you are mixing your focus from lack to abundant, back and forth, the Universe does its best to follow your focus. Can you see how this can slow the process down?

Something else that causes a time delay in applying the Law of Attraction intentionally is attachment. When all you think about and focus on is 'when, when, when is my desire coming to me,' you have just formed an attachment to your desire. And that will keep your desire at arm's length because you are creating an impatient emotion that the Universe picks up on and brings right back to you.

Finding pennies or finding a parking spot has no attachment to them. It isn't a feeling of life or death when you ask for a parking spot, so therefore you ask and look for it just knowing you'll find one and you aren't worried about it. The feeling of non attachment brings it straight to you. If you become attached, the feeling is like a rock in the pathway. So remove your rocks and just enjoy *and know.*

Focus on what you want, with joy, and just know and trust that the Universe will bring you what you want — or better. Each time you focus on your desire see happiness and see it as if it is already happened. And then thank the Universe. Build a solid foundation full of wonderful desires and let the Universe bring you what you envision *without any time delay.*

CHAPTER SEVEN

A New Way of Thinking

Intentional Creation ...

When you realize that the Law of Attraction can provide you the life that you have always dreamed of, you have to begin to think about what it is that you have to do in order for the Law of Attraction to work in your favor. You have always used the Law of Attraction but not intentionally and now you have a brand new slate to create the life that you want by intentional creation. Begin by thinking about what you would like to do with your life.

Sure, you want great health, wonderful relationship, loads of money, and a "to die for" career. But let's assume for a moment that you already have all of that. What would you do with your life if you had it all?

What is the one (or several) thing(s) you would do with your time? When you figure this out, you have found your purpose. Your purpose doesn't have to be helping others twenty-four/seven in order to qualify as a purpose.

Your purpose is defined by *what you could do all day long and then continue doing the next day with the same enthusiasm and joy.*

Find your purpose (of what makes you happy) and that is a good place to begin attaining the life that you so deserve and desire. When you find and live your purpose you are helping others through that purpose whether it be direct or non direct help. Your joy goes into the consciousness of the Universe and helps others throughout the Universe.

It is your job to find your joy so that you can help others. If you're not sure of the purpose then make that your visualization and ask the Universe for your purpose and just see that it comes to you in an idea or throughout the day. The Universe will bring you the answer if you really want it and focus on the joy it will bring you to have your purpose that will fill the empty space you might be feeling.

Once you have found your purpose it gets easier. Knowing what you want is just as important as visualizing on it. Begin to visualize with your purpose in mind. See that all aspects of your life are clearly wonderful because of this purpose. See that your life is steady and wonderfully easy while you are working toward your purpose.

Break down any negative repetitive patterns you may have that could be keeping you from the focus of your purpose. If you have any negative mental patterns, replace them with positive affirmations that will encourage and inspire you. Take on a whole new way of thinking about your life and you.

Begin to see what a wonderful exciting being you are and always have been. Listen to your inner self and realize that your inner self is perfect and your physical self can be directed from the inner self. Your inner self is what will give you the direction as to which way to head with your newly discovered purpose.

Take on a whole new life and a whole new way of thinking as you begin to apply the Law of Attraction intentionally. Each moment is a new moment to create a new you. Don't waste any more time investing in the old you, the one with all the repetitive patterns that hold you back. Invest your time in the new person and the new life you are creating for yourself. It is well worth it.

The Science of Thought ...

Our mind power doesn't necessarily originate within just us; our mind power originates within what is known as the Universal. The Universal, whether you call it the Universe, God, or the All Knowing, is the source of all energy and of all matter. You are the channel for dispensing this energy. You are the way that the Universe creates the different mixtures which result in the structure of all experiences.

Scientists have determined matter is nothing but a massive collection of molecules. The molecules have been determined into atoms, and the atoms have been determined into electrons. It has been determined that electrons fill all space. They exist in all places and they saturate everything. They fill all bodies and live in empty space as well. Electrons are in everything.

Electrons would eternally remain electrons *if they were not directed where to go to amass into the master collection of atoms and molecules.* The director of personal electrons is your mind. Quite a few electrons surrounding a core of force become atoms. Atoms come together in a scientific mathematical ratio proportionate to develop the molecules. The molecules join together to create many compounds that, again, join together to create the Universe.

Therefore, it goes that thoughts can actually change your world. It's pretty amazing, isn't it?

Cells are how electrons manifest in the body. Electrons have mind and intelligence enough to carry out their jobs in the human body. Each and every part of your body is made up of cells. Some of the cells work alone and others work together as a group. The cells are taking care of different functions throughout your body. They each have a collective purpose. Cells are also living life forms. So that being said, there is mind in every atom of your body. This mind that is in every atom is the subconscious mind. The power of a person to think and control the subconscious mind is the conscious mind.

The subconscious mind lies in every cell of your body and it acts without our conscious knowledge. The comparison between the subconscious mind and the Universe is like a drop of water and the ocean. The subconscious and the Universe are the same but differ like one drop of water to the ocean. There is only one degree of difference between the two.

The subconscious *is the connecting link between the Universe and the conscious mind.* When you consciously suggest thoughts (your desires through visualization and affirmations) to the subconscious mind, the subconscious mind will automatically put it into action. And because the subconscious is one with the Universe, there are no limits that can be placed there. That is how the subconscious and the conscious and the spirit are all connected, and that is why the Law of Attraction is so perfect.

The spirit self is the part of you that is always connected. The spirit self is the part of the All that is always connected to the All. And thought is the invisible link in which we as human beings communicate with the Universe. Thought is the magic that brings a human into a being that feels, knows, and thinks. Vibration is the action of thought. The vibration is what goes out and attracts the right supplies that are necessary to create your desire. Thought and vibrations are both amazing things. Thoughts are what create everything. Thought is what connects us to the All and, as we said, is our means of communicating with the Universe.

We can only see what is already living in this world. But did you know that when you visualize, that visualization already exists in the spiritual world? And if you want it in this physical world, you must concentrate and train yourself to think of it often and with great joy.

When you visualize, know that whatever it is already exists in the spiritual world. You're not making it up. It has already been created *there*, so when you begin to doubt the actuality of your desire *remember that it is already created.* You just have to get it into the physical form *here*. Visualization is a form of imagination. When you think, you form images and impressions on your mind and they turn into concepts and ideals that then turn into plans that become your future. So how do we control our thoughts?

Thinking is creating a thought but how it turns out is based on its quality, intensity, and structure.

The quality of your thought depends on the substance that the mind consists of. If thoughts are created from the ingredients of strength, joy, and determination, then the thoughts will be directed by those qualities.

The intensity of the thought depends on the feeling in which the thought was infused with. If your thought is positively constructed then your thought will have an intensity and vitality that will grow and expand it. Your thought will attract to it everything needed to complete your desire. If the thought is negative or hurtful, however, it will seed discord.

The structure will depend on the images that you emit. It depends on the impression you create, and how often you think of it; of how clear your vision is.

If you have one thought of a particular want this week and then you are unfocused and change it again and again, you are scattering your forces and your result will be a chaotic mixture of all that you thought of, not your original desire.

When scattering your thoughts the subconscious mind doesn't know which direction to go and the results will be all over the place. When you become sidetracked by other things, your focus will naturally go to whatever sidetracked you which creates vibrational distraction. This is a sure way to attract what you don't want.

Don't lose interest in your primary focus. Instead, see whatever it is as being accomplished. If you stick to what you desire and concentrate on it with joy (knowing that it is already here for you), you will have no problem attracting your desire.

As late as the 1950's could anyone have ever imagined that we could conquer outer space flight? Somebody *thought* so! When you focus your mind on the problems of life, think about what that does for you. So can you imagine what would happen if you instead decided to focus your mind on the solutions of life and what that would do? Just a thought!

The Core Being . . .

We've discussed how to handle all your physical world desires but there is a very important part of all of this that you can't forget about, and that would be your inner self or, as we call it, the Core Being that resides within every human. The Core Being has everything to do with applying the Law of Attraction.

Everything that you do, you create from your inner you. The Core Being is the one directing your physical self but if you allow the physical self to stand in the way, you will have a life of unintentional creation.

You have a physical self, a subconscious self, and the self known as the Core Being. The physical self is what you work through in order to get the job of life done. Your subconscious self is the automatic pilot. It is responsible for keeping your body going and managing any thoughts that you may focus on. It automatically takes care of your breathing and it keeps your heart pumping, and all the other functions of your body working. It repeats the process over and over again to where it all happens without you even thinking about it.

Think enough on disease and your subconscious will pick this up as a repetitive thought pattern and it will be created within you in some kind of form — whether it is mental or physical. The subconscious is also responsible for repeating the thought processes that you are constantly creating.

When you think on and feel a 'focus' of some sort, and you repeat it over and over again, the subconscious picks up the repetitive behavior and it goes on automatic pilot until you decide to change it to something else.

The subconscious causes the automatic repetition in your life and the physical self is what you use to experience what you are create and focus on, whether you do it intentionally or not.

So who makes the decision to create your life? It is you and we're not talking about the physical body; we're talking about the eternal you, the Core Being within you. And the Core Being is who you really are.

The inner you, the Core Being, knows everything about you and understands why you do what you do no matter what it is. It approves of you, unconditionally loves you, and accepts you no matter what.

The Core Being is connected to the All of life, the Universe. No matter what mistake or failure you think you have had or are responsible for, the Core Being understands and will do its best to guide you.

Sometimes we don't listen to the wisdom of the Core Being and try to live only as the physical self which can be ego driven, fear based, and insecure. It can make decisions within your logical mind that seem right but never get you close to the life that you want. The logical mind and the physical self can get in the way of what you want.

So how can you get beyond the physical self and live through the eyes of the Core Being within you? Live through the inner you and project this inner you onto your physical life. Whenever you are making a decision ask your Core Being for the answer and then listen.

You will be able to feel or hear what will give you the most joy. If anything comes from fear or insecurity, this is the logical mind speaking. The logical mind is constantly trying to caution you but the Core Being will only give you thoughts of love and direction and not fear. Know that you are guided and expect to be guided.

If you live and think from your Core Being you will be living and thinking from unconditional love, only approval and acceptance, and when you genuinely feel these emotions, your life can only be full of unconditional love and all the wonderful feelings that emit from the inner you.

When you focus on what you want in your life, focus from the inner you and you will be able to see a clear path of how to go about achieving the life that you want. It can happen instantly or it can take a little time to let go of the logical thinking and think from within, but once you do, life will change.

By listening to your Core Being and quietly diverting the logical mind, you will receive clear ideas and thoughts on how to go about achieving your desires. When coming from the point of view of the Core Being, the Universe will pick up on the vibrations that you are emitting through the Law of Attraction, and it will bring it all right to you without the interference of the logical mind.

Now don't go swearing off your logical mind altogether. Your logical mind is a wonderful tool communicate through and to think and to help carry out the automatic piloting, but sometimes it just has a mind of its own that may stem from many generations of family insecurity, or your own perceptions that are in fact misinterpreted through the logical mind.

When you live from within, the misinterpretations diminish and you will be able to see the whole picture and not just a small portion as the logical mind can do.

Where You Came From . . .

Where did we come from? Isn't this a book on positive thought?

What makes us think we know where we came from? After all, there are so many religions and beliefs out there; what is the truth?

In actuality the basis of all beliefs and religions are the same. That love and its existence is what are constant. Everything that we experience always comes back to love. Every decision is based on what we want or don't want, what we like or don't like, and it always comes back to what we think we love or don't love.

The Universe is a pure energy that is based in pure love. Whatever you believe and what 'feels' right to you is your truth but the only truth that is constant for everyone is Universal love.

Religion is a man-made belief, its pure intent being love. It is when man gets involved that the intent is morphed and changed. But whatever the religion, you must know that fear is not a natural state of the hereafter and neither is punishment. You judge yourself, not the Universe. You realize what could have been done differently when you return to your eternal self minus the physical vessel.

This is our truth.

Through listening to the higher self we feel we know where we came from. We come from the Core Being plane which is also called the hereafter, other world, or whatever comes after this physical life. This Core Being plane is a wonderful place full of love, of helping, and learning.

Each being is a spark off the divine, the Universe, and the understanding that is there is amazing.

Time doesn't exist like it does here in the physical world. Every moment is the past, present, and future depending on what you decide. Many things are not even humanly possible to fathom because as humans we seem to limit what is possible. In the Core Being plane there is no doubt or fear so there are no limits. Even here there are no limits but our logical mind can't comprehend that sometimes.

There are a group of enlightened beings that help you with your physical outline as well as others who want to help you with your physical journey just as you help them. An outline is drawn up of what you want to know and experience and there are certain key moments in your physical life that are predestined.

Sometimes we get so wrapped up in the process of physical life we ignore what we are being told within. We ignore the reason we came here in the first place. It will become much easier when you begin to see the deeper meaning in situations and do your best to listen and learn.

Lessons and experiences can all be positive if we begin to not 'fight' ourselves and begin to 'listen' to the direction to go. This in short is what we are here for.

You become more enlightened and you obtain more knowledge as well as becoming closer to what and who we truly are. You choose it. You choose your own time to head back to the Core Being plane with all your new knowledge and understanding. You chose your 'check out' time before you came here. You chose your 'weaknesses' and handicaps to enable you to help others learn through your experiences.

The enlightened beings there are proud of everything you do to learn and grow. You are a hero or a heroine just for deciding to come to the physical plane.

Removing Mental Patterns . . .

You are comprised of every thought and perception that you have ever had and continue to have. This includes every thought and belief system that your ancestors had whether they are alive or have passed on, and every societal thought that has crossed your path that you have paid attention to. This is what makes each one of us so different and so special; there are no two who are alike.

What you choose to accept (or not accept) into your world can make a huge difference when attaining the life that you desire. You may have repetitive mental thoughts that are yours but actually stem from the belief of an ancestor that has long since gone, yet the mental pattern still lives within you.

Even if you have a direct perception of another completely from their viewpoint, you will either accept this viewpoint or not. When you are a young child, you receive many views that make you who you are today and you may have accepted a belief system without ever knowing why. It has become one of your repetitive mental patterns. You may also have adopted a belief and morphed it into something completely different than what it actually was intended to be.

Direct your wants and desires and actually achieve what you want to create in your life. But first you want to examine your repetitive mental patterns and keep the keeper and rid yourself of the ones that could be stopping you from actually attaining your desires.

When you flush the ones you no longer need, it's important to assign a replacement mental pattern to fill the void of the one that is no longer there. When you begin to think of the old pattern, you'll want to readily replace it with the new mental pattern. This will take some practice but it is worth it because at that point you will be well on your way to achieving your dreams through the Law of Attraction. But make sure you remain steadfast and refrain from sliding back into your old repetitive mental patterns. It is so easy to do when you first begin changing to reflect what it is that you truly want to attain.

Grab a notepad and write down all the things that you feel are problems in your life; the ones that you would like to change making sure to list your feelings about these challenges and why they've become a part of your life.

Let's say that your goal is to enjoy a career that you love while earning more than enough money. Write this down. Then ask yourself why you think you can't attain it. Perhaps your answer is, *You have to work a nine-to-five job and get paid what they give you. Life isn't about fun.*

Where did this mental pattern come from? Did you hear your dad say it over and over again when you were a teen, or maybe from your great grandpa who struggled through the Great Depression and never quite got over it?

When you pinpoint the source of the pattern that you aren't happy with, change it and note the change next to the old mental pattern. Drill it in your head (figuratively speaking, of course!). Know your new mantra forward and backward and the next time you experience a moment when you don't think you can possibly accomplish something, you'll have your new mental pattern established, ready to serve you much better than the negative repetitive pattern ever did. With the change of a few habits (and that's all they are: *habits*) you can be the person you truly want to be, and have all the things that you ever dreamed of.

Confidence . . .

How do you feel about yourself? Are you concerned about what others think of you or are you worried about what opinion someone may have? Confidence problems happen when you are so worried about what someone else may think of you; when you worry about what others will think of you this only attracts more people and situations that create more false self-opinions.

How do you end the cycle? How do you gain the confidence to make your own decisions without worrying about what others may think? How do you 'not care' when you actually *do* care what people are thinking and possibly saying about you?

Here's a mantra to stick on the refrigerator door that you should live by:

Don't be who you think you are, be who you wish to be.

Let's take that a step further in order to understand exactly what it means. Don't be who you think others think you are; be who you want to be, not what others tell you who you are.

It sounds easy and, believe it or not, it is. Think about it. Is it important to care what others think of you? If it is important, then why? Is it going to be the end of the world if someone doesn't like you? Is it just the 'end all be all' if someone looks at you the wrong way? It only feels like it is the end if you let it affect you.

Think about the freedom of not worrying about what others think of you. How can you gain some of that freedom? By allowing others to have their perceptions of you and by not buying into what they apparently believe.

Who knows you better?

Have those other people ever walked in your shoes? Could they possibly know what it is like to be you? So why do they have some strange power over you that makes you feel that you need to even care what they think? You have the freedom to create who you want to be. No one can change that.

So who do you want to be?

If you could create all of the qualities you imagine for yourself, what would they be?

Would you be happy as that person that you just created? And assuming you became this person you created, does it still matter to you that you'll likely have the same amount of detractors offering up more negative opinions?

Be who you wish to be; be that girl or guy who is the one *you* would admire and who is happy with life. Start being that person now. You can assume the traits of the person you desire right now.

See yourself as that adventuresome hang glider surrounded by friends who truly appreciate you for who you are; a wonderful human being.

Take a look in the mirror. Look yourself right in the eyes and tell yourself, without looking away, what you like most about that person in the mirror. If there are qualities that you wish to possess, tell yourself how great it is to have those qualities. You may feel like you are 'faking' it at first but your subconscious doesn't know the difference between the real and the 'fake' so keep telling it what *you* want it to know until you feel the shift.

You will become the person you wish to be. Your former self will merge with this newly confident person. Hold your shoulders back and walk with confidence. Even if you don't feel confident, by taking the confident walk, your body receives those signals. Others will begin to notice your newfound confidence and in turn *you will feel confident.*

When you understand that your world is the only world you should create and that everyone else is creating their own worlds, you can choose to be either an actor in their 'play' (their world) or be the lead role in your own play called life. The more attention you put toward another's perceptions or opinions, the more they will become a part of your own reality. You are the one who is in control of it.

Once you have gained the confidence in yourself and know exactly what you want to be and have no doubts, the Universe will bring people to you that will compliment your own confident vibrations. It is always in how you see the world that creates the reality of your own world.

Is the Law of Attraction Selfish?

Wondering if the Law of Attraction is selfish is like asking if it is wrong to be happy. All that anyone wants in life is to be happy, and everyone has different ways of creating what they define as a fulfilling life.

Some of us choose to explore the Law of Attraction to help us learn to live in joy, and at the same time make our lives more worth living by attaining what we desire along the way. But how can your happiness help others in the world?

Happiness is contagious. When you make a conscious decision to be happy, and when you are able to see life as a wonderful gift that you've been given, you begin manifesting what you desire in your life. Others see this as it occurs, and that inspires them into action.

Even your reluctant spouse or partner can see how joyous you have become and decides that he or she, too, will 'live' life. Then the kids see that Mom and Dad are nice and relaxed these days and are actually laughing more, and even playing.

Your sister and her family drop by for a visit and are curious to know what has happened. *They* want to know what your secret to happiness and success is. Soon her husband and she get on the band wagon and create a more fulfilling life for themselves.

Do you see how if happens? When you make a conscious effort to enjoy life you have positively affected the lives of others. But you don't just stop at your spouse and family. You do it to the grocery store, at work, at the video store, and soon your infectious joy will create and spread more joy in and through others.

The helpful and giving spirit you possess becomes contagious. People demand to know your secret and become more at ease as you continue to live in ease. Tell us how that can be selfish?

Positive thought is one of the most giving attributes if you openly practice it. And the fact that you will receive the same kind of treatment is the wonderful side effect of giving to others.

The groups accusing practice of the Law of Attraction as being selfish just don't understand the LOA or how it works. When someone doesn't understand something, they tend to pick out the points they think they understand and then tear the concept apart from their perspective. In reality they are creating the very reality that they want and it doesn't include knowing that we determine the direction of our own lives through thoughts and feelings.

Some prefer the use of another means to their own truth and your truth likely conflicts with theirs. This is where your own sense of self should step in and realize that everyone has a truth of their own and that it is important to allow others to be who they are even if you don't agree with their way of thought, just like they should offer you the same courtesy.

Many people can't fathom that it could be as easy as 1-2-3 to start having a life of joy, living the life that they desire through something as easy as the Law of Attraction. Being happy isn't selfish. Being happy will help everyone around you. The ultimate goal is to live your life and be happy while enjoying the process. Enjoy life as you want it to be and the rest will fall into place.

Answers are Within You . . .

Wouldn't it be wonderful to have a friend who could tell you all the answers to all of your problems? And wouldn't it be nice to have this friend answer every question you ever had and also gave you advice that was just right for you? Wouldn't it be nice to know exactly what to do in any situation?

What if we told you that the friend is you.

Every answer to every question in the world lies within you. You are not the physical being you think you are. You are a part of a consciousness that already has all the answers, and you can access all those answers with just a little patience and focus.

To find your answers arrange some quiet time and trust in yourself and the Universe. First sit by yourself and think of the questions that you would like the answers to — whether general or a specific question that pertains to you.

Get comfortable and clear your mind. If your mind begins to wander, gently coax it back. Close your eyes and concentrate on your breathing.

Ask your Core Being the question either silently of out loud. Continue to sit quietly and just listen. You may hear something immediately or it may take a few times to hear the core being whisper to you. You don't always get an answer when you are sitting by yourself. You may get your answer hours later in the car.

Be aware of what is around you so that if the answer arrives in an unconventional way you, will recognize it. The Universe has some very unique ways of imparting the knowledge that you seek, so be on your toes.

And know that when you ask for an answer, the answer is already there. It just has to assume a physical form that you will connect with.

For example, one time we were searching for a particular kind of brown manila envelope for a project we were working on. We had gone on a 'bean hunt' for these elusive envelopes.

The next day, when we were in the office, one of our co-workers told us about a new Mom and Pop office supply that had just opened up. "They have great stuff," she said.

We went to the local office supply and the envelopes were there. We asked, didn't push, and remained aware. The answer came quickly. You just want to look for the signs and take action. The answers are within you and they always have been.

Releasing Negative Experiences . . .

One day we received a call from a young lady who got us thinking about getting to the root of a problem, and then letting it go.

She was upset that a guy she was interested in was playing an immature game of trying to make her jealous. Not only did it not make her jealous, it actually angered her. She said that at work the next day, all she could think about was how upset she was about the incident and so she called us to find out how to let the situation go.

When something upsets you, first examine the real reason you're upset. Remember, when you are upset it always comes back to you and your thoughts and feelings. The root of the problem is usually right there within you and while it may take some searching, you can find it.

The young lady said she couldn't think of why it upset her, which is what upset her the most. We asked her if perhaps it was because the guy that she thought he was turned out not to be what she wanted. She said that wasn't such a big deal; that she knew there were other fish in the sea. So we went a little deeper.

Was she upset with the fact that he actually made her jealous, or was she upset because he had figured how to upset her? She went silent, and that's when we knew we hit upon the root of the problem. This particular guy had figured her out first, and it upset her that someone she barely knew could press her buttons so quickly. She felt unprotected and insecure. That was her problem. She realized why she was upset: She felt vulnerable and someone took advantage of that feeling. Now was the time to let the situation go. Now it was time to find the solution.

So, she was vulnerable. Big Deal. We suggested she not put up her defensive walls, but instead work through the fact that she can be vulnerable — and that is totally okay. This was about her, not about the guy. In fact, he was a long forgotten part of the equation. Once she figured out that it was all about feeling insecure, she no longer felt that way. By figuring out what the root of the problem was, it no longer seemed scary. She was able to shine light on the problem.

Her solution: Realizing that there are many fish in the sea and that the positive qualities that this particular guy *did* have, can be found in someone else who doesn't come with the need to make girls feel insecure. In actuality he was the one feeling insecure and he was creating his world, and she merely became a part of it. But only for a little while.

Once she figured out that she didn't want to be a part of the world that he was creating, she became empowered and felt more secure than ever.

Finding the source of the upset and letting the situation go is a freeing experience. You no longer become attached to the situation or put energy toward it, and by letting it go you are no longer a slave to the negative feelings and thoughts that are connected to the circumstance. In other words, you won't be attracting more of the same.

Secrecy . . .

Have you ever had one of those days when everything was just right? The whole day just seems to be gelling, and you feel great. You tell a colleague about your incredible day and the "well-meaning colleague" says something to you that just hits you wrong, and it makes you feel bad about yourself. So the rest of the day you begin to doubt yourself. The one remark just throws your day off.

Now you've entered a state of doubt and soon the feelings of lack set in. This one person, who had no idea that they put any doubt in your head, changed your day. Your feeling of doubt really is your responsibility, whether you accept the remark or not, but this kind of event can throw your thoughts and feelings into a space you don't want to take them.

This is a reason to keep your enthusiastic thoughts and feelings to yourself while you manifest what you desire. If you are the kind who isn't affected by someone else's thoughts, then go ahead and shout. But if you're like most of us, there will be someone who can throw a wrench into the mix and get you off kilter.

Many famous inventors kept their thoughts and feelings about their inventions to themselves while they were in the process of creating them. Wilbur and Orville Wright, Alexander Graham Bell, and Thomas Edison (just to name a few) had initially told many about what they were inventing but people couldn't appreciate what they were creating for mankind. They were pegged as crazy, but as we all know the inventions they created changed the world. When they heard what people were saying, they stopped talking about their inventions.

They would work deep into the night so no one would see what they were doing or ask them doubtful questions or offer them unsolicited opinions. If they had taken those opinions to heart would they have made less incredible inventions? They learned early on to keep silent and create until the creation was physically manifested. Even then others didn't think what they did was possible. There will always be people in the world who doubt. It's our responsibility as Law of Attraction practitioners to remember that the others who create doubt in your mind don't understand what you have found in the Law of Attraction. And their opinions only affect you if you allow them to.

You are like the great inventors of the world, creating a wonderful physical manifestation for your life. So if others affect what you think and feel, then keep it quiet. Be like the great inventors of the world and believe in and build your dream without the sideway glances of others. You can achieve this by being silent.

CHAPTER EIGHT

The Past

Yesterday is a Closed Book . . .

If we change our outlook of our past experiences, is it possible that our desires will come quicker to us? Your past experiences are a direct link to what you are experiencing today.

We each have past experiences that affect our lives. When we think back on some wonderful thought from our childhood, we feel secure and happy. But when we focus on a past experience that was traumatic, we feel insecure and upset.

The more focus you put on a particular thought and feeling, the quicker the Universe will attract what you are emitting. We can't impress this upon you enough.

When you focus on anything for a period of time, the subject of your focus begins to engender a life of its own. The Universe takes its cue and brings what you are focusing on.

For example, let's say that you had a traumatic relationship as a young adult. Even though you are older now, you still reflect upon that experience. It was a time that was hurtful to you so every time you find yourself returning to that one terrible experience. But the more and more you think upon and relive the trauma, the more you will attract that kind of experience back into your life.

Why do you think people tend to repeat negative behavior patterns? They continue over and over again to relive past experiences, and when you do that, the Universe sends more of it to you. The Universe isn't being unkind; the Universe is just fulfilling its job. It's taking its cue from you through what you feel strongly about.

So how does one stop the repetitive thoughts and feelings? By starting anew as often as you have to. Yesterday is a closed book. You don't have to relive past experiences.

When you think of a past experience that may not have been a pleasant one, do your best to separate yourself from the experience itself while learning what you want or don't want from that experience.

Find what you feel you may have learned from the experience and what you would or would not do again. How might you have done things differently and what could you have done to change the outcome?

After you have dissected the experience through impartial observation instead of from emotion you can let it go much easier. It served its purpose *but you can let it go.*

If you find it isn't so easy for you to let go, then play this game with yourself: When that traumatic experience surfaces in your memory, change the experience to what you *would have wanted it to be.* By doing this, you can change your focus (as well as your feelings) to the positive and create better days for the future.

By changing the past, even if it is only within your mind, something miraculous happens. Your heart becomes freer because of the hope of what could have been, and you create wonderful feelings about a situation that was once such a negative focus for you. When you create those great feelings, by focusing on the joyous moments and gratitude now, you will bank good feelings that the Universe will work towards bringing to you. When you close the book of Yesterday, especially on the past's not so great experiences, you will find that life becomes much smoother and easier.

And what about the wonderful experiences from the past? Such past experiences are good ways to get the 'happy' thoughts going. Use the experiences for the good feelings you can generate from them now.

What we do is this: We take a past experience and capture the *feelings,* not the experience itself, and then transfer the good feelings to what we currently want out of life. By using this method, you will have a great emotion attached to a current-day-focus that will become your true experience in your future.

Use this method to release the hurtful past and then concentrate on a beautiful tomorrow for yourself and your loved ones. Each experience of your life is created by you. You create sometimes from the Core Being within yourself. But other times the physical ego can step in the way and do its best to create from the material physical sense. When anything is created from the ego it usually comes from a need to be appreciated and approved by others. The puffery involved is usually because in some way you feel you have to be patted on the back. How about patting your own back and not worry about others and what they think of you?

Forgiveness . . .

Do you have someone that you have a hard time with? Maybe someone who is always late every time you see them? They end up being at least an hour late no matter what.

You have a hard time forgiving them for being late and you start to build resentment. All these strong feelings are signaling the Universe to bring you a resentful feeling. As we know, not forgiving someone can actually slow down the process of obtaining what you want through the Law of Attraction.

Beth relates:

"Fourteen years ago a traumatic experience happened when someone tried to strangle me. The hardest part of this experience was that it was a family member (by marriage) who tried to end my life. At the time, he was on testosterone and had an undiagnosed bi-polar/schizophrenic condition. But even so, this incident traumatized me and my then eleven year old daughter.

"We handled it as best we could while getting restraining orders, going to the doctor, filling out police paperwork, and taking my daughter to a counselor to help her through the scary experience of seeing her own mother strangled. I had been sheltered by my parents all my life and nothing like this had ever happened in our family. This was no time for forgiveness.

"This incident happened before I understood the Law of Attraction and forgiveness was definitely not on my list. My brother-in-law went to jail and I figured my sister would leave him after she saw what he was capable of. I didn't need to forgive him; he wouldn't enter into my world ever again. I was wrong. He served his time and my sister went straight back to him. This was something that I would have to deal with. He wasn't leaving my life and I decided I was not going to be around my sister or her husband ever again.

"Not long after this incident I began searching for answers in my life and found many teachings of positive thought. There were answers there that felt like my truth that I had been seeking. Here was the answer to attaining what I wanted in life. I learned that I had to deconstruct who I was and my belief and behavior patterns and build brand new ones. This was going to be exciting. Then I realized that I was going to have to deal with 'the incident' and somehow rid myself of the feelings I was harboring.

"The incident had left me feeling angry and hurt. My sister hurt me by going back to this man and I was angry with myself for not fighting back. I was hurt from the mental anguish it had caused my daughter, and me, not to mention the physical pain I had endured after the attack. I felt like this man had taken some of my personal power away. So applying the Law of Attraction, while harboring all these feelings, was going to be an issue. I knew I had to lose the feelings and the only way I knew how was through forgiveness.

"You see, it isn't just about your forgiveness of another. When someone hurts you, it isn't just you. It is your spouse, your children, your parents, and anyone else who is close to you. When you have all those strong angry and hurtful emotions it affects everyone. Not to mention instigating more emotions of fear.

"Apparently my brother in law got help for his bi-polar issues and he stopped the testosterone. This made it a little easier for me to remotely consider forgiveness. Who does the forgiveness help? Out of anyone, it helps the victim. Because once you forgive, you are no longer a victim. I decided that I was going to forgive him, but not the act. My logical mind could handle a little forgiveness for him but not for what he had done.

"This was a start, but let me tell you this. When I completely forgave the act and the person, I felt like a new woman. I no longer felt like a victim. I felt like I took my power back and not only that, I felt like I fought back by forgiving. When I released all the hurt and anger and decided I didn't need it anymore, I could see clearly once again. He had nothing on me. It took a little time to release the welled-up emotions but over time, I did. I actually had learned from the experience. I spiritually grew through the process. I learned much more about myself than I ever had and it helped me to release feelings and thoughts that I had been hanging on to.

"No more anger flashes, no more hurtful flashes. I 'let go' of this situation because I am no longer about the woman who was strangled.

I am much more than that, and in order to get past that traumatic experience, I had to forgive *for myself* so that I could move on.

"When you don't forgive someone, you are only hurting yourself. All those angry, scared and hurt feelings are keeping you from being all that you can be in life. It doesn't mean that you have to hang out with the offender, but it is important to get rid of those strong negative emotions; the ones that could be keeping you from your desires when too much focus is put toward the negative emotions."

Do you have someone you want to forgive? It is freeing to forgive another, no matter what hurtful act was done. By truly forgiving someone you can move forward in your life.

Get beyond 'the incident' and 'let go' of the strong negative feelings. Concentrate on who you really are and concentrate on your wonderful life minus 'the incident', whatever it happens to be. Don't let it be a crutch enabling you to feel bad.

Blame . . .

Being responsible includes knowing that you have created all that is in your life up to this point. Life is not meant to be a blame fest in any way — there is no blame. In fact, blame is just another one of those 'lack' words that is useless in the end.

Blaming is just living in the past and not keeping your eyes on the present. Regret is also a negative form of living in the past. It's fine to look back and examine what you have learned and experienced so that you can enjoy the experience even better the next time.

There is nothing wrong with improvement. But regret and blame are extremely strong, self-defeating emotions that really teach you nothing. And remember that when you blame others, you are really blaming yourself.

We have a family member who, no matter what is happening in his life, complains and blames. Whether he has a good day or a bad day, he lets everyone know how bad his life is, and it continues to turn out just as he says. He lets you know about every person in his life that has let him down. Everyone else is responsible for all of his woes.

No matter what you say to him, no matter how much you try to lean him toward thinking that life isn't so bad, he just gets frustrated and tells you how the world is going to end. He revels in blaming everyone else for what he calls his rotten life.

Usually when we have a family get-together, he is unable to make it. He blames it on his car, or on his boss, or on his wife. It's actually a kind of visualization joke with us. About a couple of weeks before we have a family event, we start visualizing a calm, serene, positive, and fun-filled family get-together.

We wonder if our certain family member will have gotten himself into a better space. We include our bemoaner in our visualizations but he doesn't show up. He can't stand to be around that many happy people.

We would love nothing more than to see him happy but we are not responsible for making him happy and are not responsible for creating his world. *He* is responsible for making his own happiness and creating his own world.

There are a lot of people who blame others for the current state of their lives. Unless we're speaking of a child/parent relationship how can someone else be responsible for another's life?

It's a hard pill to swallow but if you have a bad day, you are the one who created that day. It's not necessarily intentional, but all the same you do create it. It is usually created from past images and feelings that you previously emitted and have returned as your 'now'.

Take responsibility for your feelings and what you are focusing on and create each day, the kind of day that you would like to live for the rest of your life. Take responsibility when you find yourself blaming someone else in your life. Every action and every feeling that someone has toward you is a reflection of what you are or were feeling.

You attracted this person or situation because of a feeling you were sending out to the Universe. Understand that changing your perception of others and loving yourself will attract more good things into your life.

It can be hard to believe that you somehow created your Aunt Suzy's report, telling you that she saw your girlfriend with another man, and it can be hard not to blame Aunt Suzy or your girlfriend for your misery.

But somewhere you were creating the vibrations that accompanied that scenario, whether it was that you were afraid of losing your girlfriend, or didn't trust her, or you just outright felt bad. Blaming the other players in the scenario will not help your circumstance.

Does this mean you have to ignore your pain when hurt by someone? No, just make sure that you stay clear of blaming and take responsibility for your own life.

Change it to a life that you are happy with. There is only one person who is responsible for your happiness and that is the person you see every morning in the mirror.

Non Judgment, What a Concept!

We are all about comparisons as human beings. Everything that we see and hear we make a comparison of some sort. Even as simple as seeing a color. When we see the color red we know it is red because we make a comparison to another color by saying, *That is a red flower. Red is this color and not blue.*

We begin making comparisons from the second we come out of the womb. When a baby begins to eat solid foods, it already has likes and dislikes. Likes and dislikes are making comparisons. Part of this process is when we make a comparison we begin to point out what is 'right' from our point of view and what is 'wrong'. In actuality, right and wrong are only perceived by society of what is right and wrong. When you see someone walk down the street have you ever looked at them and instantly decided you liked or disliked them? You are making some kind of comparison from your own perceptions.

Maybe she reminds you of an old girlfriend that you can't stand. Or maybe he puts you in mind of your favorite Uncle Ralph and you take an immediate liking to him.

Whatever the reason we make judgments all day long. So what would life be like without making judgments on other people let alone situations that we assume we know what happened? How can your judgment of what you experience cause life to slow down?

When you focus on judging another person you yourself will experience that from another source in your life. Every judgment you make isn't going to make a difference in the Law of Attraction, it is only the judgments that produce some kind of emotional response within you that will either speed up or slow down what you focus on.

Let's say you go to the grocery store and you decide which produce you are going to pick. You decide on oranges this week. You don't have any emotional attachment to the choice you made so this particular choice isn't going to affect your focus of what you want. Now let's take a look at the situation when you make a judgment and we'll see how it can cause the end result of what you want to take a detour.

So you go to the same grocery store and select the same oranges. As you shop you see a couple arguing with one another. You overhear that she is angry because he only chooses items that he wants to eat and never considers her. You immediately make a judgment about what a jerk the guy is without really knowing either person and not knowing the whole picture. Maybe you begin to sympathize with the woman and wonder what it feels like to be her and maybe you have even experienced a similar situation. This is where your judgment will affect what you emit in vibrations. Your judgment may make you upset which is an emotional response and this triggers negative emotions in you that attract more of the same.

Think about how many times a day this happens to you. When you're at work or standing in line where you can observe people, you might look around and make a judgment. *I don't like her dress. I think he looks rude. She isn't talking very nice on the phone. I wonder if she is cheating on her boyfriend.*

These thoughts can cause your own mind to go places that cause a negative emotional response. Being judgmental can cause you to think that you are much better than someone. Or maybe you degrade someone in your mind in order to make you look or feel better. This is the worst kind of judgment. It only hurts you in the long run. You are attracting back to yourself whatever you think and you speed up the process by what you feel.

Do yourself a favor and try being non-judgmental about your surroundings. You may not like what others look like or do but you should not make the judgment. Let others be who they are and respect the fact that they are creating their own reality.

Don't make your reality a part of what they do or say merely because of what you think about them. Focus on what you want in your life and focus on what you are creating. You don't need to be worried about what others are creating. If someone asks for your opinion or advice give it to them without judgment and leave judgment of all things and people behind you.

Live the Day in the Now, not in the Past . . .

You hear the words 'live in the now' and wonder how you can possibly live the life that you want with the lack of material things you believe it takes. So instead try feeling what it is like to live how you want to live. You don't have to buy anything to 'feel' how you will feel when you have all of your desires. The things that you want are just that... *things.* Yes you want those things but *why* do you want those things?

Do you want to be successful because you will feel safe and secure or otherwise feel good about yourself? Do you want money because you want some relief in order to feel secure without financial worries for you and your family? Examining why you want the things you do is a good place to start.

Live the day feeling safe and secure as if you already have everything you desire. Live the day free of stress as if you already have the relief that you seek. By doing this, you are indicating to the Universe that you are living how you want. If you feel safe and secure, you will attract the safety and the security you seek along with all the things you want attached to it. The material things are just a byproduct of what you really want for yourself.

Live each day through your feelings as if you have it all. Continue to visualize and focus on what you want in the end but also make sure that you 'live the feelings' of what you want now. Live each day as if you have it all. Be kind to others, help others, enjoy the day no matter what kind of day it is, always find the positive within the negative, and trust in the Universe to bring you what you desire.

By enjoying the day without reacting to everything around you, you will attract all that you are feeling and thinking to yourself. If you react in joy and in kindness, you will have a life filled with joy and kindness. Live each day by enjoying and giving to others. Give a smile. Give with a laugh. Give with listening to someone who needs to be heard.

Live each day in ease. When you wake up in the morning, say to yourself, *Another day of ease!* and go about your day. When something comes along that upsets you, calm down, and say to yourself, *The day is with ease...* and continue to move forward with ease.

Believe it, know it, trust it, and feel it, each and every day, and the Universe will continually bring you the life that you want. One of the keys to the Law of Attraction is to live life as if your visualizations have already come true. You can do this through feelings that you can generate while envisioning the life you want.

We all have desires and when we get those desires fulfilled we will still have more desires; we never stop creating. Live the feelings of what you want to come into your life, and live them on a daily basis.

Letting Go . . .

You had every intention of having a wonderful day when you woke up this morning. You step on something that was left on the floor and there isn't any hot water. You reboot yourself and say, *I will start the day again and I will have a good day.*

Then you go downstairs and the cat has been sick leaving little 'gifts' all over your white carpet for you to clean up. Your husband asks if you are having a hard morning. You make a big production of cleaning up the cat accidents as you growl to your unsuspecting husband, *Yes, Dear.* **I am** *having a hard morning.* Your hubby smiles and tells you to just let it go. The feelings... *just let them go.* Then he offers to make breakfast. Do you know that's all there is to it? The situation stays and builds if you let it but if you just let it go it leaves.

Isn't it amazing what can happen to your day and to your life when you decide to just let situations or things go? It truly can be that easy. Letting go gives you the chance to start over again, as many times as you want. Why hang on to the angry frustrated feelings when letting go can make them all go away?

Letting go provides a feeling of freedom unlike any other. Let go of the pressure before the day begins to turn. Situation after situation can be released avoiding the burden of a bad day. When you try to control the situations around you and seem to be fighting against an invisible force, the act of letting go breaks the hold.

Are there any situations that you can let go today? If the barista at the local coffee shop gets your coffee wrong for the fifth day in a row, just send the coffee back and then let it go.

Don't relive the situation over and over by retelling every colleague in the break room. You are only confirming that it will happen once again. Just let it go. Laugh! Big Deal. You will be amazed at the results as your life moves forward.

CHAPTER NINE

Using Negative Emotions Constructively

Can Anger and Worry be Good Things?

We were given thought and emotions and while it is our choice whether we use them for positive or for negative, why even have negative emotions? It is not realistic to say, "I don't get angry or frustrated anymore since I found the Law of Attraction." Even the best of us will encounter negative emotions from time to time.

Part of being human is having a range of emotions that tell us whether we are in a positive or negative frame of mind. We have the choice of which particular thoughts and feelings we want to live with. So how can anger or frustration actually help us when using the Law of Attraction? Surprisingly, it can motivate into a whole new way of thinking and growth.

The goal in having all these different emotions is to use them constructively and with balance, not to eliminate them. Anger can be an obstacle that can keep you from what you want and can stop you in your tracks but it can also be a stair-step to spiritual growth. The answer really depends on you. Sometimes amazing results can come out of anger.

When a parent learns that a child steals and then becomes upset about it, this tells the child that this is something they mustn't do. They learn the proper way to treat another individual. Such intense emotions can change another's life when constructively used in this way.

Obviously when you are upset with your child, after the initial upset, calmly give them direction. They will understand that it isn't right to hurt another by witnessing your initial reaction, but they will also learn that you love them no matter what they may have done as you find a solution that will help your child understand.

By explaining the scenario and letting them see how whatever the transgression was hurt someone, they can begin to understand the true picture that resulted from their actions.

How about when you are frustrated and angry about a particular event or situation in life? Maybe it angers you to see homeless people on the street and through that anger and injustice comes the motivation for you to do something about it. It is the *anger* that can motivate and then put you in a space that makes you happy to help.

It is when anger stays around and doesn't do any good that it causes harm to you and the people around you. Being angry for anger's sake hurts you and the others around you. Take a look at your anger and frustration to see if they stem from your own ego. Are you angry because someone maintains a different opinion than you? Are you upset that someone doesn't take your advice? Are you angry because deep down inside you may feel inferior and therefore feel the need to lash out?

Discovering the source of your anger is important to diffusing it. If it comes from your own ego it is you who needs to work on those feelings; not the person you are lashing out at. When you don't use anger to motivate in some kind of creative way, you are merely directing the anger outward and this can be destructive to both you and society. Look at it this way... anger has the ability to create or destroy.

When you come to terms with the anger and let it go and you discover that you can still be happy in the midst of a tumultuous situation, the angry feeling lifts and you feel lighter because you are vibrating at a higher level.

Pinpoint where the negative feeling is coming from, recognize it, and move forward. Direct the anger constructively. Let it motivate you and allow you to make positive changes; first, with your own thoughts concerning the circumstance, and then to the circumstance itself.

Do something about the situation. Let anger be the catalyst to inspire change and then transform the anger into solutions and begin creating what you want from there.

Getting Beyond the Negativity . . .

Start with trying to observe the negative thoughts instead of 'buying into' them. Sometimes it can be hard to catch a negative thought before it comes into being within your mind. Do your best to catch any negative thoughts when they enter your mind, and just for a moment step aside and observe your own logical mind and why you are having that particular thought.

Observe instead of participate. Is the negative thought stemming from a legitimate worry or does it arise from some insecurity within you?

Get to the bottom of the thought and break it down. Don't become frustrated that you have negative thoughts. We all have them. It is our reaction to them that is the difference. Take whatever is negative and transform it into a positive. Catch yourself at the outset and either transform the thought or completely negate it. When are in the habit of negative thinking you can negate it by making the effort to catch yourself and observe what the thought is really about.

Keep this in mind the next time you tell yourself that your negative ways aren't hurting anyone. *They are hurting you* and that's enough to be concerned about, right there. And don't forget that your family has to deal with your negativity as well.

We attract those around us who are of like mind but when it comes to family it's different. We signed up for them in order to help them through this life just like they volunteered to be with us. Your negativity or your positive outlook affects those close to you and if you have children, they are always living by your example. So make sure you recognize what you emit on a daily basis. And it isn't enough to just get rid of the negative in your life.

It is important to replace the negative with a positive. When your logical mind starts to disrupt the negative patterns, it must have something to replace that void. If you don't replace the negative pattern the mind will head right back to where it was... in the negative zone.

Observe your own thought patterns throughout the day and see where your focus heads the most with the negative. Write it down and when you have the chance, write an opposite to that negative. You will find that life will take a positive turn for you once you are able to keep most of the negative thoughts that creep in from time to time at bay.

How Can I Feel Abundant When I'm Not?

How many times have you said to yourself, "Today is the day that all my dreams come true" and then the day passes? You see little progress with the Law of Attraction in your life even though you are intentionally watching each thought and are living in the now.

First of all, remember that just because you can't see it doesn't mean that the Universe has forgotten about you. You are in a constant state of movement as you decide what you want and don't want. You are always moving forward even when you don't feel as if you are. You are always experiencing and learning in this lifetime.

Step out of your box... the box that says that what you think is going to happen and use some tools to break through the lack of abundance. When we're talking abundance, we mean money, relationships, health, career, and anything else you can think of that you would like an abundant share of.

Draw a picture, cut out pictures, make a list of the life that you want and use childlike wonder to feel the life you desire. This exercise sends vibrations out to the Universe that in time becomes a repetitive habit of the mind. See abundance in your everyday life. See it as if it is the air that you breathe. Abundance is in all things that are available to you. When you breathe in, breathe in abundance in your mind. You can do this exercise anywhere. No one will even know. Take a deep breath and feel the abundance that surrounds you.

Next, *look for abundance.* Find it in your everyday life; in the trees, the sky, through laughter, love, even material things. See that there truly is no lack of abundance in anything. When you understand that and can realize that you deserve it, and that it is for you, abundance will arrive at your door.

And what is the *best* way to attract abundance into your life? Be thankful for what you already have in your life now. Be appreciative of where you are today as you focus on what you want tomorrow and recognize that every experience has a purpose and a growth element for you. Look within at what you may be learning through this amazing process and thank the Universe for the helping you there.

The Contrast of it All . . .

You know what you don't want but do you know what you *do* want?

Isn't it funny how when you ask a group of friends what restaurant they'd like to eat at, they can immediately tell you where they don't want to go, agreeing on where to go seems to take forever. It's great to know what you don't want and that is half the battle. But deciding on what you do want can be a bit tricky.

When applying the Law of Attraction it's important to focus on what you want. Wherever you place your focus is what will come to you. Just a few minor adjustments of your thoughts and feelings will point you in the direction that will lead you down a positively driven path. Are you focusing on the *do* wants of your life? Do you see the hope within what you want? Can you see the unlimited possibilities to your life? You don't have to know exactly what they are yet but just know that they are there. You do have the ability to change your life just with your thoughts and feelings.

Let it Come to You . . .

Are you working so hard, visualizing, meditating, pushing, pulling, and doing everything you believe you can to manifest your dreams into the reality of your life? Do you figure that by constantly putting more attention toward it — and giving it your all — that it will bring it to you all that much faster?

You may want to rethink this. Just how do you go about getting what you want in your life without having to push it into existence? By letting it come to you. This doesn't mean that you sit back and do nothing but it does mean that you have to release all those self imposed deadlines that you have placed on your goal. Instead of working against the clock, instead sit back and enjoy life as it comes while the Universe takes care of 'how'.

When the Universe taps you on your shoulder and reminds you that it's action time, you mobilize for whatever action is required. This process can happen with ease as long as you see it that way.

Part of the process of getting what we want is the "getting there" and if you are enjoying the journey you are already creating more moments to enjoy and draw upon. How can you guarantee that your dreams will come? By living each day expecting they will come and remaining in a space of total gratitude.

See all the joy that you can find in your life right now. Make a mind shift recognizing that you are thankful for each and every situation even if you're not sure why. When you can live in that frame of mind and visualize your life with ease your dreams will come.

Take hold and begin to focus on everyday life and you will soon be on your way to the life you want to live. Your inner you knows what you want to do even if you don't yet know.

It will be revealed to you when you are ready to hear it, so get ready by living in positive thought. Be ready to take action and don't go chasing your life but instead let it all come to you with ease through your own positive thoughts and feelings.

Taking Care of the Inner You . . .

We remember the days when we were always trying to catch up, constantly feeling as if we were always chasing down our dreams and our lives. Time would seem to get away and we felt like we never had enough time to get it all done. This was before we found the knowledge of what life is really about, and when we finally did, things began to change.

You see, all the rushing around and trying to get it all done was attracting more of the same; the ever vigilant Law of Attraction was in motion as it always is. We just weren't aware of it yet. When we became tired of the rat race and listening to others' opinions of what our lives should be, we went searching for the real answers. We knew there was more to life than working at a job we didn't want to be at, and a life full of chasing.

Over many years, finding and studying what we felt was our truth, we began to see that even though we are physical beings we are also a spiritual being and it was important to pay just as much attention to the inner self as we gave to physical outer self. When we're told to take care of ourselves we tend to focus on activities like exercise and eating right without giving a second thought to our inner selves.

We take for granted that we breathe in and breathe out without even thinking that maybe the inner self has functional requirements, too. Your physical being would not exist without that inner self that keeps in mind the journey you agreed to take before coming to this physical world. It keeps you focused on what you wanted to experience and grow through here on earth.

How it all comes about fits into the sphere of free will but the inner self has everything to do with what you do here. Your inner self should be taken care of at least as well as you take care of your physical body.

Your inner self needs nourishment or you are liable to become an unbalanced being which gives you a distinct disadvantage in creating the life you want through the Law of Attraction. So how do you feed your soul? Many people feed it through religion and prayer and others through inspiration.

Many feed it through watching a wonderful movie, listening to music, or reading a great book. However you feed it is up to you. How you feed your spirit should feel joyful and refreshed after. If you don't, if how you feed your soul leaves you with feelings of doubt or fear, then you need to develop another way.

Meditation is a positive way to connect to the inner you, as well as visualization. This places you in a zone where anything is possible; and, you are then working with your logical mind as well as the spirit mind in order to manifest your wants. It gives you a chance to step away from the current reality and instead create the reality you truly desire as long as you are passionate about what you focus on.

By feeding all aspects of yourself you will find that life will become more balanced, less hectic, and you will feel like you are moving forward instead of standing still. You will find that fear and doubt leave your life as you connect with your inner you.

Balance ...

It is quite a feat to be able to balance daily physical life but now we're going to suggest that you also begin thinking about balancing your mind, body, and spirit. It's important to be a well oiled machine when focusing on what you desire.

We take time as human beings to make sure we eat properly and exercise well. We visit doctors and take medication for what ails us. We down vitamins and herbal supplements to prevent anything from going wrong physically but how well do we take care of our mental and spirit states?

How exactly do you take care of those? To take care of the mental body it is important to feed it with thoughts of what will make you happy. Do you feed your mental body with joy, compassion, and love or do you give it a constant diet of fear, doubt, and control?

Taking care of the spirit body happens through the meditative state. Sleep is not just a way of nourishing our physical bodies. Sleeping is the time for the spirit to soar and go places while the mental and physical bodies rejuvenate.

The spirit self, your Core Being, knows that it is connected to the Universe at all times and this is the reason it is important to connect through meditation, sleep, or some other kind of quiet reflection in order for it to gain the sense of being connected in the physical body.

Balancing all three of these isn't necessarily difficult, but many people leave out one and tend to overdo it on another. We're sure you've met people who exercise 24/7 right but haven't got a clue why they are so stressed out? They have overdone it on the physical level and have completely ignored their mental and spirit bodies. They are feeling the imbalance.

Have you also met the kind of people who don't seem grounded? They may not pay too much attention to their physical bodies and only speak of the spirit world; they seem a bit out there. *They* are overdoing it by living only in the spirit world.

How about the one who only pays attention to the physical, material world and all they care about is achieving their material desires through the Law of Attraction? These folks haven't got a clue as to how to make it work since the only thing they can focus on is the material world.

Transformation . . .

Some believe that all one has to do is think positive and everything will arrive on their doorstep. But there is a transformation that happens in someone when they embark on the journey of intentionally creating their life. They usually begin with the material wants of the world; the 'perfect' relationship, 'perfect' health, and the 'die for' career. And usually, there are three ways in which people will go.

One is to try and live like they want without working on the self. Then they can't understand why it all doesn't come rushing to their door, returning to their old ways because it is so much easier to live life uncomfortably comfortable.

The second way is to dabble in positive thought and know that everything in theory works, but still not make an effort to really see what they can truly do. Again, because everything else gets in the way and it becomes 'too hard' to have to search within one's self to attract the life they wish for.

And then there is the third way. These folks realize all they are creating and search within to change negative patterns. And something happens when they realize that we are completely taken care of; that we are each having a physical experience here, and that we are unconditionally loved.

Soon the material wants seem to disappear as they begin seeing with true eyes, and are able to realize that each moment is another moment to create and to love. This is not to say that they don't care about any kind of physical wants, it just means that they consider how minor the physical wants are compared to what life is really about.

In all three circumstances the Law of Attraction is working, bringing what is focused upon.

Finding the meaning to your life is just as important as getting that new car because when you are at peace and happy within yourself, you will become a changed person. And that is truly what life is about.

CHAPTER TEN

Set the Stage for Miracles

They Happen Every Day . . .

Could there possibly be a way to have miracles come into your life everyday? There is when you bring the Law of Attraction into the equation. When you expect a miracle, you receive a miracle and that is just about as simple as it gets. Expect and Receive.

Miracles happen everyday, but some we just don't see. The sun rising, the flowers blooming, the birth of a baby are all miracles and when you begin to see what kind of miracles are part of your everyday life, you will begin to take notice of even more miracles in your life. Take a moment and think about every miracle in your day, from the fact that your body just automatically works, to how the sun rises sets each day. By focusing on these miraculous events, thoughts, and feelings, you will start to enjoy your own life miracles.

We were on a deadline one day and everyone in the office was diligently working while enjoying lots of fun talk and mirth, when one of the servers went down. You should have seen the look on our faces, what with a looming deadline.

Each one of us took a look at the computer and tried to help solve the problem. Working in our office is quite something because even though we are all card carrying Law of Attraction practitioners, some can fall off the wagon when it comes to a crisis of this proportion.

Our newly hired receptionist said it first: "Well, guess we should expect a miracle, don't you think?" We all looked at her and released a sigh of relief. We all knew that no matter what, our job was to trust the Universe and expect a miracle. So we did. Sure, there were some iffy moments, wondering if it would all work out.

We had called our computer man but he was out on calls and wouldn't be in for the rest of the day. We were going to have to wait until the next day which would have put us way behind schedule, but we kept the faith and knew that even if we were delayed it would work as it should. In the meantime, we expected a miracle. Anytime anyone brought up something about the downed server we would remind him or her that it didn't matter because a miracle would happen.

We were the last two out the door when who should call? Our computer repairman. "Just took a chance you might be there. I had a cancellation and wanted to know if I could come by right now?" MIRACLE. And yes, the server was fixed in minutes.

We wrote the words, "Thank you Universe for the miracle" and left it up on the board for all to see in the morning.

Expect a miracle. It may come when you least expect it, or in a different fashion than you thought, but it will come as long as you expect, focus, and release it to the Universe by using the Law of Attraction.

Cycles . . .

Everything is not about the Law of Attraction but everything is about positive thought. No matter what you can be positive in any situation. This is not to say that you won't get upset at times but it does mean that after the initial 'blow up' you want to get back into the place of positive thought.

You cannot solve any problems through confusion or anger because the intense negative feelings put you in the place of seeing only problems and not the answers.

Another rule of the Universe seems to be cycles. You can look at many different parts of the Universe and see that it runs in cycles. The moon cycles from waxing to waning and back again. There are four seasons that cycle and return each and every year. The sun comes up and the sun goes down. The ocean tides ebb and flow. These are just a few examples of the cycles in the world. We, too, experience cycles.

Of course you've heard the phrase, *When it rains it pours*. This is always something that seems to happen in our lives. When you have a wonderful windfall in life more seems to come; same with a streak of bad luck.

We are affected by many things in this life but the steady constant is 'how' we think. If you are able to ride your own cycles and keep your focus on what you want through positive thought, the negative cycles that seem to affect your life won't be unmanageable. Going with the flow of life instead of fighting tooth and nail is how you get through those moments in life that can seem less than grand. Know that those moments will pass.

Your positive thought will get you through life's trials that can seem overwhelming because any negative times you may be encountering are only temporary. The cycle will change because it always does, and you have the power to put your focus where it belongs. Not on the problems of your life but on the blessings.

Many promise that when their problems are all over, *then* they will see the blessings. It doesn't work that way. It is when you recognize that what you have right now is the blessing; that the problems will dissipate as you count these blessings now as you envision the blessings of your future.

Visualize Your Miracles . . .

In order to attract miracles, you must dedicate a time for yourself so you can envision what you want in your life. Whether you use visualization for a solution to a problem or for your life dreams it is an amazing feeling once you get the hang of it. It is a miracle in itself!

Find a location where you won't be disturbed and can come return to anytime you wish to be by yourself. You can play music or use whatever helps you relax but your visualization time should happen with absolutely no distractions.

Before you begin, make sure you have already thought about what you want your visualization to be. For instance, maybe you want a brand new car with a brand new house and a wonderful mate to share this with. Or maybe you have a problem at work with a co-worker that you want to solve. Just have the general image available for yourself.

Now sit in your designated quiet spot, in a comfortable position, but not so comfortable that you fall asleep. We can't count how many times we have gotten so comfortable that both of us would wind up snoozing! Breathe in and breathe out through your mouth. And with each exhale relax your body even more than it already is. Keep this up until your mind feels clear of the world and you feel relaxed. You can close your eyes or leave them open. We tend to build better images with our eyes closed but others like to look at some kind of collage they may have created to remind them of the situation they want.

Build that image within your mind. See yourself in that new car, driving to the new house. Feel the air in your face as the car moves, smell the flowers as you pull up the driveway to your new home, and feel the hug from your mate. Hold this visualization in your mind as long as it will stay with you, and should a moment of doubt suddenly appear, it is time to stop until the next time.

This may seem like a silly exercise but it is far from that. The images you build are living energy. Thoughts and ideas begin in the spiritual Core Being world and the more focus you put on them the more real they become until one day you will see a physical manifestation.

Visualization is a wonderful tool to focusing your logical mind on the positive of possibilities. If you practice this enough the subconscious will begin to pick up the repetitive nature involved and do it on its own. You will find when you engage in daily visualization it will become easier and easier which is a sure sign that the subconscious is assuming a new repetitive pattern in your life.

The Wandering Mind . . .

How many times have you been in the middle of visualizing when your mind takes on a mind of its own and begins to wander? It jumps from the image you are focusing on, to an image that has absolutely nothing to do with your visualization. Your mind offers opinions on what to do about everything; everything but what you are trying to focus on and put energy towards. And before you know it, visualizing on what you desire becomes the last thing on your mind.

Let's get you on the right track with visualization. If you are visualizing the same picture every night and day, they can soon become both repetitive and boring for you. When practicing the Law of Attraction, it's important to see and feel what you want through visualization, but only if you are truly feeling whatever it is.

If what you believe you desire has become boring? With a complete lack of feeling or negative emotion, change your visualization to something that makes you feel joyful. Even if it may be something different from what you were previously visualizing. So get creative.

Here's another thought.

Sometimes your own logical mind can have a hard time believing that it can have everything it desires. It tells you all the reasons why you couldn't possibly have what you want — *period!* An easy way to stop the logical mind from telling you it just can't work is to generate visualizations that the logical mind can understand and *could* possibly manifest now. Here's an example: A client of ours kept having problems with concentration through her 'quiet' time. As we deconstructed how she was visualizing, she would sigh repeatedly. When we asked her the source of her sighs, she told us that she couldn't believe that the Universe would send her $100,000 this year. Even though she wholeheartedly believed in the idea of the Law of Attraction, she couldn't imagine that this money would come to her. So we suggested that "For right now, just right now, until you get comfortable with the numbers, tell us what is believable to you?" She thought for a moment and said, "Ten thousand dollars."

Then we asked, "So you believe ten thousand dollars can come to you right now... even tomorrow?" She responded that, in her opinion, it wouldn't be a problem at all. "Then visualize *that* number," we suggested. She protested at that point that she wanted much more than ten thousand. We suggested that she begin visualizing on ten thousand until money started coming in, and then reminded her that when her logical self saw what could happen, it would be easier to visualize even more money.

Make sure to visualize what you do with the wealth, as well. When you begin to feel how great it is to be taking a vacation with your family, and staying in the grandest of hotels, this evokes feelings of wealth. Remember, you have to believe that your desire is real, and that it is there for you now. If what you envision isn't something you feel can happen, create a smaller picture until you are confident enough to know that you can have it all.

If you have a particular important day on your horizon — or any day for that matter — spend a few moments seeing the *end* of the day first. Create how you want your day to actually be by 'reflecting' on the day that just started. See your meeting going exactly as you wanted it to, see the checks that came in the mail, and don't forget to thank the Universe. By thanking the Universe before it happens, this tells the Universe that you know that it actually will. Visualize the end of the day the first thing every morning, and you will begin to see your days merge into the exact picture that you intend.

When you are having 'one of those days' where you just can't concentrate on any form of visualization, then don't. Just sit still, clear your mind, and reflect upon thoughts of peace and happiness. This will bring many more you peaceful and happy moments from the Universe. This will connect you with the All that Is.

By just quieting your mind you are moving closer to attaining your desires. This is the time when some great insights will arrive, as well. When you get back in the mood, ready to visualize, pick up where you left off. It is important to make a daily practice of visualizing and meditating. You are connecting with the Universe and others through this time.

Clarity will come from this practice and will help you to make choices that will head you in the direction you have been focusing on. We can't say enough about how important this is. Even if you don't visualize, daily meditation is a must.

When you are visualizing it doesn't mean that you have to sit in one spot. You can visualize anywhere and imagine the circumstances that you wish to be in. When you come home from a long day at work, you can imagine your life exactly as you prefer it and just become what you desire.

For instance, if you would like a new home with brand new rugs and furnishings, then when you arrive home from work, envision that your current home is entirely the new home you that desire. The new rugs are there, the bank account is golden, and your mate is right there next to you, just as happy and content as you are. Give it a try. It can be a load of fun to take a look in your closet and imagine all the new clothes complete with tags ready for your south pacific cruise.

Something that is important to remember is if you encounter the wandering mind monkeys while visualizing, don't beat yourself up over it. Each moment is a new moment to create and to start up again. The more you visualize and let the mind chatter pass, the more proficient you will become in releasing the chatter.

You're giving your logical mind something positive to do. You are retraining your own mind to focus on the positive for a short time. Be patient with yourself and even if you can only manage a few moments without the mind chatter you are ahead of the game.

Material Things: A Byproduct . . .

"I'll be happy when..." How many times have you said this or heard someone else say this? *"I'll be happy when I have everything that I want in my life. I can't wait to have happiness."*

It's true when they say, "Money can't buy you happiness." Even though many who want the material things in life believe that money is what they really want, it isn't true. What most people are after is a sense of security — to not have to be worried about anything material in life. By having things and money they believe they will feel safe, secure, and happy.

Listen, you can have the career, the relationships, the money, the health and the wealth to be happy if you'll do just one thing... that is, *to just be happy.* It isn't the other way around. Happiness comes from within. It doesn't come from the wants that you envision. Even when you are envisioning the life you desire you are including happiness in your picture. Being happy is a state of mind and in order to attract it you must begin with it.

But how do you find happiness in the life you have at this moment? Recognize what an incredible experience life really is. Look around you. There is so much to be happy for. Shift your focus from what you think you *don't* have and shift it to what you know you *do* have.

Are you happy within? Are you *really?* Do you ever lie to others as a way to make yourself look better in their eyes? Do you not trust others, or care too much about what they think?

Being happy within means accepting and loving who you are no matter what 'weaknesses' you believe you may have. Did you know that everyone has something they don't like about themselves? That is because we have been taught to make comparisons of our own lives against the lives of others. Yet each and every one of us is the same; we all have differences and similarities. Who said these are weaknesses? They are just another aspect of whatever our physical vessel happens to be. We are all the same within.

When you can begin to realize what a blessing it is to be alive and to experience this wonderful life, this is when you will find your happiness within.

When you realize that you are always connected to the Universe and are never alone; that, through the Universe, you always have a cheerleading team boosting you on. You'll see that there is no risk, that there is nothing to fear, and that there is self acceptance. That is when you will find your happiness and will then begin to reflect happiness in every direction of your life.

Giving Back . . .

Furthering your own growth and helping others in any way with your passion and purpose should be your goal from now on. Ask yourself honestly if that is where you are coming from. Does your current life reflect those thoughts? Create, learn, and evolve your own spirit, help others from the place of wanting to help others and not because you expect something. Give from an open heart, never expecting a thing in return.

This doesn't mean that you have to go out and give so much of yourself that there is nothing left for you. It only means that you treat others as you want to be treated and to give freely of what you do have to offer. Basic Golden Rule stuff.

Is it a smile? Maybe it's an e-mail sent to someone who needs to know that someone is there who cares?

Any way that you give will return to you in a way that is meaningful to you. Giving back is being thankful and appreciative to your fellow man. Make sure to give back to yourself as well. Enjoy each day and treat yourself with respect. Never forget that you are a loving spirit of the Universe that deserves to live as you want to in this physical lifetime.

Problem Solving as a Changed Person . . .

It takes new thought to solve a problem. To solve a problem, you can't use the same mind as before. In order to solve problems you have to think large and expect change. If you have a repetitive problem you have to think differently in order to solve it once and for all.

If you focus on the problem you will attract more problems to try and solve. When you focus on the solutions the answers arrive. Thinking differently just takes you and only you. And try your best to avoid the perceptions of others.

When you're able to get out of the limited box, the Universe can bring you many conventional and unconventional ways to any solution. Just be aware of what the Universe is sending to you.

Remember, your thoughts and feelings are powerful and how you choose to direct them reflects where your life will go. That's our promise to you.

About the Authors . . .

Beth and Lee McCain have authored numerous books on the subject of the Law of Attraction and positive thought, including **A Grateful Life: Living the Law of Attraction, Transcripts from the Core Being** and **Unlimited Thoughts.**

They also appear in the motion picture, **Beyond the Law of Attraction,** and host the popular weekly radio program, **RADIO L.O.A.** The happily married couple lives in the serene Alsea Valley near the beautiful Oregon coast.

This book was digitally printed on acid free,

65 percent recycled paper, and set in 11 pt.

Palatino Linotype

————

Named after 16th century Italian master of calligraphy Giambattista Palatino, Palatino is based on the humanist fonts of the Italian Renaissance, which mirror the letters formed by a broadnib pen; this gives a calligraphic grace. But where the Renaissance faces tend to use smaller letters with longer vertical lines (ascenders and descenders) with lighter strokes, Palatino has larger proportions, and is considered much easier to read.

————

Thank you for purchasing this book; we sincerely hope it was of value to you, and that it was and continues to be a source of encouragement for you as you Walk Your Path . . .

3055698

Made in the USA